French Literature: A Very Short Introduction

VERY SHORT INTRODUCTIONS are for anyone wanting a stimulating and accessible way into a new subject. They are written by experts, and have been translated into more than 45 different languages.

The series began in 1995, and now covers a wide variety of topics in every discipline. The VSI library now contains over 500 volumes—a Very Short Introduction to everything from Psychology and Philosophy of Science to American History and Relativity—and continues to grow in every subject area.

Titles in the series include the following:

AFRICAN HISTORY John Parker and
   Richard Rathbone
AGEING Nancy A. Pachana
AGNOSTICISM Robin Le Poidevin
AGRICULTURE Paul Brassley and
   Richard Soffe
ALEXANDER THE GREAT
   Hugh Bowden
ALGEBRA Peter M. Higgins
AMERICAN HISTORY Paul S. Boyer
AMERICAN IMMIGRATION
   David A. Gerber
AMERICAN LEGAL HISTORY
   G. Edward White
AMERICAN POLITICAL
   HISTORY Donald Critchlow
AMERICAN POLITICAL PARTIES
   AND ELECTIONS L. Sandy Maisel
AMERICAN POLITICS
   Richard M. Valelly
THE AMERICAN PRESIDENCY
   Charles O. Jones
AMERICAN SLAVERY
   Heather Andrea Williams
THE AMERICAN WEST Stephen Aron
AMERICAN WOMEN'S HISTORY
   Susan Ware
ANAESTHESIA Aidan O'Donnell
ANARCHISM Colin Ward
ANCIENT EGYPT Ian Shaw
ANCIENT GREECE Paul Cartledge
THE ANCIENT NEAR EAST
   Amanda H. Podany
ANCIENT PHILOSOPHY Julia Annas

ANCIENT WARFARE Harry Sidebottom
ANGLICANISM Mark Chapman
THE ANGLO-SAXON AGE John Blair
ANIMAL BEHAVIOUR
   Tristram D. Wyatt
ANIMAL RIGHTS David DeGrazia
ANXIETY Daniel Freeman and
   Jason Freeman
ARCHAEOLOGY Paul Bahn
ARISTOTLE Jonathan Barnes
ART HISTORY Dana Arnold
ART THEORY Cynthia Freeland
ASTROPHYSICS James Binney
ATHEISM Julian Baggini
THE ATMOSPHERE Paul I. Palmer
AUGUSTINE Henry Chadwick
THE AZTECS David Carrasco
BABYLONIA Trevor Bryce
BACTERIA Sebastian G. B. Amyes
BANKING John Goddard and
   John O. S. Wilson
BARTHES Jonathan Culler
BEAUTY Roger Scruton
THE BIBLE John Riches
BLACK HOLES Katherine Blundell
BLOOD Chris Cooper
THE BODY Chris Shilling
THE BOOK OF MORMON
   Terryl Givens
BORDERS Alexander C. Diener and
   Joshua Hagen
THE BRAIN Michael O'Shea
THE BRICS Andrew F. Cooper
BRITISH POLITICS Anthony Wright

John D. Lyons

# FRENCH
# LITERATURE

A Very Short Introduction

OXFORD
UNIVERSITY PRESS

# OXFORD

UNIVERSITY PRESS

Great Clarendon Street, Oxford ox2 6DP

Oxford University Press is a department of the University of Oxford.
It furthers the University's objective of excellence in research, scholarship,
and education by publishing worldwide in

Oxford  New York

Auckland  Cape Town  Dar es Salaam  Hong Kong  Karachi
Kuala Lumpur  Madrid  Melbourne  Mexico City  Nairobi
New Delhi  Shanghai  Taipei  Toronto

With offices in

Argentina  Austria  Brazil  Chile  Czech Republic  France  Greece
Guatemala  Hungary  Italy  Japan  Poland  Portugal  Singapore
South Korea  Switzerland  Thailand  Turkey  Ukraine  Vietnam

Oxford is a registered trade mark of Oxford University Press
in the UK and in certain other countries

Published in the United States
by Oxford University Press Inc., New York

© John D. Lyons 2010

The moral rights of the author have been asserted
Database right Oxford University Press (maker)

First published 2010

British Library Cataloguing in Publication Data

Data available

Library of Congress Cataloging in Publication Data

Data available

Typeset by SPI Publisher Services, Pondicherry, India
Printed and bound by CPI Group (UK) Ltd, Croydon, CR0 4YY

ISBN 978-0-19-956872-7

# Contents

# List of illustrations

# Introduction: meeting French literature

The heritage of literature in the French language is rich, varied, extensive in time and space, and appealing both to its immediate public, readers of French, and also to a global audience reached through translations and film adaptations. The first great works of this repertory were written in the 11th century in northern France, and now, at the beginning of the 21st century, French literatures include authors writing in many parts of the world, ranging from the Caribbean to Western Africa, whose works are available in bookshops and libraries in France and in other French-speaking countries. For many centuries, French was also a language of aristocratic and intellectual elites throughout Europe.

## What is 'French literature'?

Both 'French' and 'literature' are problematic terms. What are the boundaries of 'French'? Historically, the effective domination of the 'French' language among the population living within the boundaries of today's 'France' was realized only at the end of the 19th century, when universal schooling brought the language of Paris and the elites to the speakers of such tongues as Breton (*Brezhoneg*) spoken on the Brittany peninsula, Basque (*Euskara*) on the southwest coast, varieties of Occitanian (*Lenga d'òc*) such as Gascon and Provençal in the south, and Alsatian

(*Elsässerditsch*) in the northeast. Moreover, there are many important authors who have written and now write in French who do not live within the borders of the European territory known as 'France', though in many cases they are citizens of France (the residents of Martinique, Guadeloupe, New Caledonia, and so forth) or of former colonies of France such as Quebec and Senegal. Some authors whose first language is not French have chosen to write a significant portion of their work in French, for instance Samuel Beckett. Other authors, born in France and French citizens, have chosen not to write in 'French': Frédéric Mistral, like Beckett a winner of the Nobel Prize in Literature, wrote in Provençal. As for 'literature', the current use of the term dates from the 19th century, when what had long been called 'poetry' or *belles lettres* was amalgamated with other writings such as memoirs and essays as the basis for literary studies in universities. It is a bit flippant, but useful, to think of literature as what we read when we do not have to – what we read without immediate, circumstantial purpose.

## The protagonist as starting point

To get one's bearings in French literature means, in part, to have some idea of the major texts of the evolving tradition and a sense of how they relate and respond to one another. Coming into that tradition can be, at first, disorienting. Fortunately, perhaps, the situation of having to relate to an unfamiliar society and of having to determine one's own place while observing other people is a central topic of some of the principal texts of the French tradition. Whether by their choice or by circumstance, the protagonists of many French texts find themselves in situations of opposition to, or isolation from, most other members of their society. This is often a literary device for authors to make critical, polemical, or didactic points (and French literature can be called justly a literature of ideas), but it may also be a source of emotional turmoil that offers the reader an *experience* of empathy, rather than a purely intellectual insight.

It makes sense to look at literary works in terms of their central characters, or protagonists, since throughout history, epics, tragedies, short stories, and poems have very often taken the name of the protagonist as their title, whether it be *Beowulf* or *Hamlet* in English, or, in French, *Lancelot, Gargantua, The Misanthrope, Chatterton, Consuelo, Madame Bovary*, 'Le Mauvais vitrier' (The Bad Glazier), *Cyrano de Bergerac, Nadja, The Story of O*. But even in works that do not feature the central character's name in the title, the focus on his or her characteristics, thoughts, and actions makes the protagonist an obvious place to start an exploration of the literature. And it should be noted that the term 'protagonist' also applies to works, like many poems and autobiographical texts, in which the main figure is some version of the author ('some version' in the sense that we often assume a creative reworking of the first-person speaker, as when Ronsard embellishes or mythifies 'Ronsard' in his love poetry, or when Rousseau writes of himself in his *Confessions*). And since most works that make up the literary tradition have central characters, their study offers a convenient way to compare works to one another, within a single period or from one epoch to another.

Protagonists necessarily have problems. If they did not, there would be no story, no quest, no obstacle to overcome, no mysteries to solve, no desire to satisfy, no enemy to defeat. In the French literary tradition, moreover, the central figures often have problems of such a unique type as to warrant being called 'problematic heroes' – heroes and heroines whose very status and place in society is at stake – or even 'anti-heroes' (defined by the OED as chief characters who are 'totally unlike a conventional hero'). What kind of person is chosen as focal point of the plot and that person's relation to her or his society can tell us a good deal about a literary text and its time, whether that character is portrayed as very good within prevailing social norms or very unusual in an undesirable way. For instance, Rousseau's character 'Émile' in *Émile, or, On Education* (1762) is neither the most complex nor most believable character of the time, but

3

he presented a revolutionary model of human nature and of the consequences for childrearing.

In the pages that follow, we will meet a number of protagonists who were often controversial at the time when their stories were first told or published, but who now are central to the French literary tradition and to our vision of the epochs from which they come. We will also see, for the sake of comparison, some of the other figures against whom they define themselves by their difference. In each of the following chapters, which largely correspond to conventional historical periods of French literature, three or four representative texts will be taken up in some detail, while others will be mentioned for brief comparison and suggested for future reading.

# Chapter 1

# Saints, werewolves, knights, and a *poète maudit*: allegiance and character in the Middle Ages

The protagonists of medieval texts tell us about the worldview of the period that chose to focus on them. When a literature arose in the vernacular, Old French, as distinct from Latin, in the 11th century, the territory we call France had different boundaries and nothing like the national identity or organization we know today. We would describe it as highly decentralized geographically and politically (the concept of 'de-centralization' is itself our way of projecting backwards the presumption that France should have a 'centre') and personalized in its social organization. In the feudal system, power, identity, land ownership or use, and even the sense of the passage of time from one epoch to another, depended on the person in power in a given place at a given time. Allegiances shifted, power and wealth within the leading families varied from generation to generation depending on the skill and luck of individuals. Threaded throughout this society was an international institutional framework, the Church, that provided a kind of meta-identity delineating the southern and eastern boundaries of Europe. In this context, it is not surprising that the protagonists of literary works, almost invariably in verse form,

5

should be represented primarily in terms of their loyalty, the principal value of a feudal society.

## Lives of saints

The text that is usually identified as the very first substantial work of French literature concerns its hero's decision about the lord to whom he will be loyal. *The Life of Saint Alexis* (c. 1050) is the story of the only son of a wealthy nobleman in 5th-century Rome, who was married in his adolescence and fled on the night of his marriage, telling his bride that 'In this life there is no perfect love' (*En icest siecle nen at parfite amour*). He travelled across the sea to Syria, where he lived for seventeen years in anonymous, ascetic spirituality. But because he began to be honoured, he fled from where he was living, and setting sail, he was involuntarily carried back to Rome. He returned, unrecognizable, to live for seventeen more years as a holy beggar under the staircase in his father's house. His identity was discovered only at his death, from an account of his life that he wrote on his deathbed, but *The Life of Saint Alexis* that we read must be significantly different from Alexis's own account, which was written from his point of view. The narrative *Life* continues after this death to include the lamentations of his mother, father, and virgin widow and points towards the complexity of the project of holy heroism, saintliness, itself. His mother cries out, speaking to her dead son, 'Oh son, how you hated me!' (*E filz...cum m'ous enhadithe !*). There remains an ambiguity about whether she supposes that Alexis resented her for not recognizing him upon his return from abroad – he did not: the narrative of the *Life* makes it clear to the reader, but not to the family, that Alexis was determined not to be recognized during his life – or whether she supposes that this hatred drove him to his initial departure and animated his whole withdrawal from his family.

The poem makes it clear, in any event, that this type of heroism exacts a cost. The emotional cost is greater for those who love the saint than for the saint himself, since he, after all, has chosen his priorities. Yet while the family suffers, the community as a whole is shown to benefit from the presence of a saint, whose soul has gone directly to live with God in heaven: 'The soul separated from the body of Saint Alexis; / it went straight to paradise' (*Deseivret l'aneme del cors sainz Alexis; / Tut dreitement en vait en paradis*). The people of Rome, the Emperor, and the Pope all celebrate that they have the body of a saint, who will henceforth serve as their advocate with God. *The Life of Saint Alexis*, like many texts from other periods, is open to varying interpretations, to varying arguments for and against the values represented by the hero. Yet this does not imply that the writer of the *Life* was himself ambivalent. It appears clear that for the writer, and for most 11th-century readers, Alexis represented a triumph of Christian, transcendent values. Family ambition and sexual love are less important than large social units, such as the Church, the city, and the empire. On the other hand, this edifying reading does not prevent us from seeing similar conflicts of values in later works in which protagonists sacrifice their families, like the hero of Corneille's *Horace* (1640) or the heroine of Flaubert's *Madame Bovary* (1856), for what appears to them a higher calling.

## Werewolf – a nameless hero from Celtic sources

Werewolves, like saints, make difficult bedfellows, and yet loyalty to a werewolf is the crux of a story (perhaps meant to be sung) that appeared in a collection of verse narratives a little over a century after the *Life of Saint Alexis*. The *Lais* of Marie de France (c. 1160–80) draw on two literary traditions from within what is today France: the troubadour poetry of Provence and the Celtic oral narratives of Brittany. They were probably composed at the English royal court for a French-speaking Norman audience. Many of the *Lais* concern unhappily married women (discussions about love were pursued with great sophistication in the milieu of Eleanor of Aquitaine, who had been successively Queen of

France and of England), but one of them stands out both for the peculiarity of its title character, Bisclavret, and for showing sympathy to a husband married to a disloyal wife.

Marie points specifically to the Celtic origin of the story of Bisclavret while recognizing that her audience is French: 'I do not want to forget Bisclavret: / Bisclavret is his name in Breton / But the Normans call him Werewolf' (*Ne voil ublïer Bisclavret / Bisclavret ad nun en bretan, / Garwaf l'apelent li Norman*). The hero – simply known as 'a lord' (*un ber*), he is thus really nameless – is just like other people except for a need to shed his human identity several days each week. This metamorphosis no doubt represents the fondness of Celtic literature for magic and for permeable boundaries between humans and other living or imagined creatures. But it has often been noted that Marie minimized the supernatural elements in traditional stories that she retold, and in the case of *Bisclavret*, the hero's transformation into non-human form may simply be a way of representing ordinary outbursts of violence or times when one is not 'oneself'. Simply put, the husband's eccentricity consists of taking off his clothes and running around naked in the woods. The narrator tells us at the outset that 'in the old days, many men used to become werewolves', so that this characteristic is not in itself presented as being evil or necessarily alarming. The real problem, one that appears as a theme in texts of many other periods (such as Jean de La Fontaine's 'The Loves of Psyche and Cupid', *Les Amours de Psyché et de Cupidon*, 1669) is the absence of trust in the person one loves. He never showed her anything but gentleness, and he trusted her enough to reveal the deep secret that he is a werewolf. Yet the husband gets in return only fear and disgust. His wife steals the clothes that he needs to return to his human form, so that he is trapped in that of the animal, until the happy ending of the *lai* when justice is done. Tellingly, the husband's behaviour while in canine form, exhibiting great loyalty to the prince, is the value that assures his triumph and return to human identity.

### Langue d'Oïl and Langue d'Oc

The Old French language appeared in writing in 842 in the 'Strasbourg Oaths'. What we call Old French was the language of the north of what is now France and is sometimes called the *Langue d'Oïl* – that is, the 'language of *oui*', after the word for 'yes' – to distinguish it from the language spoken and written in the south (*Langue d'Oc*, or Occitanian, of which Provençal is the best-known dialect), where 'yes' was said as *oc*. Provençal was the language of the troubadours (*trobador* in Provençal: poets who recited or sang their own compositions) and of the *trobairitz* (women troubadours). Old French differs much from Modern French, which has remained largely consistent in written form since the 17th century. Today many French readers rely on the increasing numbers of bilingual editions of medieval poetry which present the Old French original and a Modern French translation side by side.

## Epic: the *chanson de geste*

Although the gentleman wolf of *Bisclavret* was a knight, the *lai* does not concentrate on what he did while in human form. Yet the conduct of the knight is the core of the characterization of protagonists in two other major genres of the period, the *chanson de geste* and the *roman*. In a highly personalized system such as feudalism, the protagonist's usefulness as well as loyalty was repeatedly scrutinized. Heroes sought occasions to demonstrate their cleverness and valour. In the *chanson de geste*, of which the earliest and greatest is the anonymous 12th-century *Song of Roland* (*La chanson de Roland*), military prowess and loyalty to the sovereign come to the fore. In the contemporaneous *roman* (or romance), the knight is challenged to find an equilibrium between military glory and success in a relationship with a beloved woman, as we see in Chrétien de Troyes's *Erec and Enide* (*Erec et Enide*, about 1170).

The *Song of Roland*, like the approximately 120 other surviving *chansons de geste* – literally, 'songs about the things done' from the Latin *res gestae* – concerns events during the reign of Charlemagne (King of the Franks from 768 to 814, and crowned Emperor in 800), but it was composed three hundred years after the events concerned. The *Song of Roland* recounts a battle that occurred as the Frankish army withdrew from northern Spain leaving a rearguard commanded by the hero, Roland, who is described as Charlemagne's nephew. The details, including this kinship, vary markedly from current historical representations of this rather minor battle in the Pyrenees against what are described as 'pagan' and polytheistic Saracens (in the historical encounter

1. **The Emperor Charlemagne finds Roland's corpse after the battle of Roncevaux, from *Les Grandes Chroniques de France*, c. 1460**

that was the basis for the *Song of Roland*, the adversaries were, in all probability, not Muslim).

All is magnified in *Roland*, through huge numbers, intensely gory description of combat and injuries, repetition of incidents and formulaic descriptive phrases. In an exclusively male society, the characters demonstrate their valour in fights that dismember and kill a large number of combatants at the battle at Roncevaux, but the core dilemma for the hero is actually a moral one: whether or not to send an alarm to the main body of the army, the only reasonable course in view of the disproportion of the opposed troops (twenty to one). Yet Roland refuses to call to Charlemagne for help by sounding his horn, the Olifant, as his companion Olivier urges. Roland replies, 'God forbid that my kinsmen through me be blamed / Nor that sweet France fall into dishonour' (*Ne placet Damnedeu / Que mi parent pur mei seient blasmét / Ne France dulce ja chëet en viltét*).

This heroic, almost superhuman, unreasonableness is what elevates Roland as a subject to be celebrated in song and worthy, within the epic itself, to be the object of vast mourning on the part of the Emperor and his army. And yet this pride is also a terrible flaw that leads to the death of the twenty thousand members of his detachment. The paradoxical nature of this dilemma is emphasized by Olivier's change of attitude in the course of the battle. Having at first urged Roland to sound the Olifant when there was still the possibility of assistance, by the time Roland realizes that defeat is imminent, Olivier veers to the opposite position and argues that he should not call for Charlemagne but recognize his own culpability: 'The French have died because of your irresponsibility' (*Franceis sunt morz par vostre legerie*). Through the character of Roland, the anonymous writer presents the burden of delegated authority in a feudal system, where physical strength, skill, and courage are important, but where the requirements of loyalty and individual and collective honour create contradictory demands.

# Romance

The protagonists of the romances have other problems and quite different virtues – or, rather, loyalty and honour are tested in different ways in a world in which the knight's relation to a woman is at least as important as his relation to his lord and his companions in arms. Originally, *roman* was simply a way of designating the Old French vernacular language as opposed to Latin, but by the late 12th century, it designated a type of story, in which an individual hero, through a quest, grows in virtue and self-understanding, and in which the love of a woman plays a large role. Indeed, the status of women in the romance tradition, where they are portrayed with respect and accorded great deference, is one of its striking innovations with respect to most classical models. The romances are traditionally divided into three groups by subject matter: 'The matter of Rome' (from antiquity, though more often concerning Greek legend and history), 'The matter of Britain' (from Celtic and English sources), and 'The matter of France' (about Charlemagne and his knights).

*Erec and Enide* is one of the five surviving romances by Chrétien de Troyes, whose name indicates his connection to the city of Troyes, site of the court of the counts of Champagne. While Chrétien was at that court, it was essentially ruled by the regent Marie de Champagne, daughter of Eleanor of Aquitaine. Like his four other romances – *Yvain, the Knight of the Lion*; *Lancelot, the Knight of the Cart*; *Cligès*; and *Perceval, or the Story of the Grail* – *Erec and Enide* belongs to the Celtic repertory of tales of the court of King Arthur, materials that had been translated into Latin and French from Breton. Erec, a young knight at the court, is escorting Queen Guinevere and her maidservant in the woods during a hunt when they come upon an unknown knight accompanied by a lady and a dwarf. The dwarf strikes Guinevere's maid with a whip and subsequently also wounds Erec on the face and neck. Erec is obliged to remedy this insult to the Queen, but he is not armed for battle. There is an odd echo of Roland's situation in

Erec's, since the two women and he are behind and out of touch of the company of hunters with the King. In fact, they are so far behind that they cannot hear the hunting horns, but unlike Roland, Erec resigns himself to deferring revenge until he is better armed, because rash courage is not real nobility (*Folie n'est pas vasalages*).

Subsequently tracking down the knight with the dwarf and defeating him, Erec falls in love with Enide, the daughter of an impoverished nobleman who loaned the hero the necessary arms and armour. Erec, blissfully married to Enide and living at Arthur's court, would seem to have everything and to be at the end of his story, but this is only the first third of the romance, and now the real challenge arises. Overcome by amorous pleasure with his wife, Erec begins losing his reputation as intrepid warrior. It falls to Enide to give him the bad news, 'Your reputation is diminished' (*Vostre pris en est abaisiez*). In a certain sense, Enide has lost her husband through his surrender to her. She had married a respected knight and finds herself with a besotted lover. Erec's solution is to set out, with Enide, looking for challenges in order to prove himself once again. The series of dangerous encounters that follows looks in many respects like the sort of initiatory ordeal through which a young man would pass in order to reach adulthood and marriage, but in this case Erec is accompanied by his wife, on whom he has imposed the requirement that she not speak. It seems like a regression on Erec's part: he wants to have adventures as if he were still alone and not part of a couple. However, at the crucial moment in each of Erec's dangerous encounters, Enide violates the condition of silence to give her husband important information or advice. Thus Erec and Enide prove that they can function as a couple and reconcile erotic love and knightly valour. Their last adventure leads them to encounter a couple that has failed to find this balance and have ended up cut off from the society around them, failing both in love and in service to the outside world.

# The lyric 'I'

In the texts about Alexis, Roland, and Erec and Enide, there is no doubt who is the protagonist, even though there is another figure in the text, the 'I' who tells the story. The writer, or the writer's self-representation as narrator, appears very early in French literature. Marie de France frequently reminds her audience that she has composed the story of *Bisclavret* and the stories of the protagonists of her other *Lais*, as in the opening verse of 'The Nightingale' (*Laüstic*): 'I will tell you of an adventure' (*Une aventure vus dirai*). But this use of the first person puts the poet in the position of presenting someone else's story.

Later in the Middle Ages, the poet moves to the central position as protagonist and tells her own story or his own story. In a certain sense, we could say that the poet, the person who tells the story and says 'I', is at the centre of one of the most important texts of medieval Europe, the *Romance of the Rose* (*Roman de la Rose*), a long verse narrative written in two parts: the first by Jean de Lorris towards 1230 and the much longer second part by Jean de Meung towards 1275. But in the *Rose*, the poet as concrete individual quickly explodes into his thoughts and the various psychic forces that either drive him towards the woman he loves (the 'rose') or hinder his pursuit. These forces become allegorical characters – Idleness, Love, Fear, Shame, Nature, Reason, and so forth – whose speeches and acts fill the romance, as they do the thoughts of the lover, in the literary tradition of the *psychomachia*, or 'battle in the soul', so that the writer does not appear in his everyday, concrete existence but as a kind of everyman experiencing the suffering and perplexities of love.

At the time the *Rose* was being written, the poet Rutebeuf (c. 1245–85) offered a much more concrete poetic persona when he made himself and his everyday misfortunes the subject in such narratives as 'Rutebeuf's Lament about his Eye' (*Ci Encoumence la plainte Rutebeuf de son œul*). Willing to write about the non-heroic events of his own life (such as his own unfortunate marriage – 'I recently took a wife / A woman neither charming nor beautiful'), he also creates a poetic voice that tells of the concrete happenings of his time in a world that was falling into decay. Rutebeuf had two major successors, poets who, like him, made themselves and the events of their lifetime the focus of their work. The first is Christine de Pizan (c. 1364–c. 1434) and the second François Villon (c. 1431–63). Christine de Pizan, born in Venice, came to Paris as an infant when her father became advisor to King Charles V. Much of her work takes an autobiographical form, such as 'Christine's Vision' (*L'Advision Christine*, 1405) and particularly 'The Mutation of Fortune' (*Le livre de la mutacion de Fortune*, 1403). For Christine (the use of the first or given name for this author, and many other woman writers of the early period such as Marguerite de Navarre, in preference to the surname, is a feature of the literary-critical tradition), the use of the first person singular, the 'I', in writing is itself an important gesture, or rather a construct, the creation of an authoritative voice for a woman. This is vividly conveyed in a passage of 'The Mutation of Fortune', in which Christine, become a widow, is symbolically transformed into a man, her voice deepening so that she can pursue the career of a professional writer.

François Villon, though his life was brief and his writings few, has commanded a place of choice in French letters since the 15th century, reprinted continuously since the Renaissance, when he was popularized by the poet Clément Marot (1496–1544), who recognized in Villon a precursor both in lyricism and misfortune. Villon is the quintessential *poète maudit* ('the accursed poet', or poet with endless bad luck). His mythic life, very much embellished, has been the subject of a half-dozen films, and his poems have often been put to music – in 1953, Georges Brassens recorded a musical setting of Villon's 'Ballad of Ladies of Olden Days' (*Ballade des dames du temps jadis*). A student, poet, thief, and convicted murderer, Villon may be called the first of a long series of criminal protagonists (whom we see later in the

In the poem known as the '*Balade des pendus*', Villon takes his typically elegiac stance. Here is the first stanza.

Frères humains qui après nous vivez

N'ayez les cuers contre nous endurciz,

Car, se pitié de nous pauvres avez,

Dieu en aura plus tost de vous merciz.

Vous nous voyez cy attachez cinq, six:

Quant de la chair, que trop avons nourrie,

Elle est pieça devoree et pourrie,

Et nous les os, devenons cendre et pouldre.

De nostre mal personne ne s'en rie:

Mais priez Dieu que tous nous veuille absouldre!

[Brother humans who live after us / Do not harden your hearts against us, / For if you take pity on us wretches, / God will more quickly have mercy on you. / You see us here, strung up, five or six / As for the flesh, which we have too much fattened / It is long ago devoured and rotted, / And we the bones are becoming ash and dust. / At our misfortune let no one laugh: / But pray to God that He forgive us all!]

picaresque novel). Although many, if not most, French poets have been middle or upper class, there is a persistent attraction in the lyric tradition to the marginal (perhaps precisely to compensate for the rigid social stratification of society).

Villon sets the pattern for much subsequent French poetry in which the passing of time and the coming of death are the overwhelming themes, linked to concrete details of life in Paris.

The main character, the poet, defines himself as a creature whose ephemeral existence is measured by the fragility of the world around him, as in 'The Ballad of Ladies', which gave the world the ubiquitous refrain, 'Where are the snows of yesteryear?' (*Mais ou sont les neiges d'antan?*). Despite the anti-heroic nature of Villon's self-description as literate singer living on the fringes of society (a persona very welcome to such 19th-century successors as Nerval and Baudelaire), there is much in this description that parallels the life of a saint, for the saint also lives in the constant presence of death, in abjection, and in disillusion.

# Chapter 2

# The last Roman, 'cannibals', giants, and heroines of modern life: antiquity and renewal

The Renaissance, renewing contact with antiquity, challenged French cultural identity and the identity of each individual in France. For France and Frenchness, the cultural vitality of Italy was a source of emulation and of anxiety. The odd reversal that constituted Renaissance culture meant that the recent achievement of French writers, painters, architects, and musicians was increasingly seen as out of date, while the much older literary, philosophical, and artistic legacy of Greece and Rome, being rediscovered, had an aura of freshness. In Italy, this shift had occurred much earlier, beginning in the mid-15th century with the fall of Constantinople and the influx of Greek scholars and manuscripts to the peninsula.

The French had been at war in Italy since 1494. These campaigns, continuing under François I, King of France (ruled 1515–47), intensified the importation of cultural influences from Italy. We can say that François quite literally brought Italian Renaissance culture to France when he invited Leonardo da Vinci to reside at his chateau of Amboise in the Loire valley, where the artist and polymath died in 1519. Leonardo was followed by such other Italian artists as Cellini, Primaticcio, and Serlio. The Italian influence in France was intensified by the 1531 marriage of François's son, the future Henri II, to Caterina de' Medici, who brought with her a large entourage from Florence. François also established the *Collège des lecteurs royaux* (now called the Collège de France) as an alternative to the medieval Sorbonne and appointed, often from abroad, the most distinguished scholars of Greek, Hebrew, and classical Latin to provide the means for French people to have direct textual contact with the ancient world. Towards the end of the 15th century, printing arrived in France from Germany, and the rapid spread of printing shops made books, including the Bible, available to a growing public of readers.

Two major issues of identity soon arose. The first was the nature of the French language and French culture themselves – could French rival the languages of antiquity and contemporary Italian as a vehicle of poetic and intellectual expression? And the second was the volatile matter of religion. Evangelical movements, urging direct knowledge of the Biblical text, offered the responsibility or the burden of choice to individual consciences. Jacques Lefèvre d'Étaples published the first French translation of the Bible in 1529.

## A French Boccaccio

Close to François I, there was a heady sense of opportunity and renewal. His sister, Marguerite de Navarre, encouraged and patronized the evangelical movement. She also wrote (or collaborated in the writing of) one of the most fascinating collections of short stories in the French tradition, *L'Heptaméron* (first printed in 1558, nine years after her death). The title is not the author's but was given to the collection because it has seventy stories; Marguerite de Navarre seems to have intended the finished book to have one hundred. Each of the stories centres on a person, often a woman, said to have been a contemporary of Marguerite herself. There are kings, queens, duchesses, and knights, but also mule-keepers, monks, ferry-tenders, nuns, and notaries. Rapes, murders, imprisonment, and adulterous liaisons are common, but so are scatological jokes. Often the villains are members of Catholic religious orders or servants of the King, and the characters who are cast in a good light are, frequently (it is difficult to generalize about this apparently simple but deeply complex book), those who follow their conscience and struggle against institutional abuses. Although the term 'realism' was not used to describe literature until several centuries later, the prologue to Marguerite's book makes a claim to accurate representation of the contemporary world.

Marguerite relates this claim directly and forcefully to France's attempt to define its national culture in the wake of Italian Renaissance influence. The prologue establishes a frame-narrative for the tales that follow: a group of five ladies and five gentlemen agree to tell stories that they know from personal experience to be true. In this way, the book asserts simultaneously a form of literary 'nationalism' in that it acknowledges Boccaccio's *Decameron* as its model but declares that in this, French, collection, the stories will all be true and will not be altered by rhetoric. Whether this rule is strictly followed is a matter of debate, but its statement, and other subsequent details of timing and localization in the stories, show an attempt to create a domestic literary model of realism that is closely connected with a critical attention to themes of confession, truth-telling, and willingness to assert individual righteousness against traditional Church, familial, and other social structures. In short, Marguerite's work, though it includes stories that are reminiscent of earlier storytelling traditions (the medieval *fabliaux*), emphasizes a new sense of the nation as literary milieu while it also grounds the 'truth' in the consciousness of individuals. While kings remain kings and innkeepers remain innkeepers, all of the characters of the *Heptaméron* have an equal claim to our attention.

## A new genre: the essay

The central character of Michel de Montaigne's writing is himself, and this first-person character, this *moi*, appears in greater detail than what we found in Rutebeuf, Christine de Pizan, or Villon. The *Essais* (literally, 'attempts') cover everything from digestion, sexual dysfunction, and fantasy to man's place in the universe, the existence of God, friendship, and eloquence. Coming a generation later than Marguerite de Navarre (1492–1549), Michel de Montaigne experienced the fervour of the newly established humanism (that is, the study of ancient letters) from his very infancy. His father had been a soldier in the French armies in Italy, and apparently brought back great enthusiasm for an uncorrupted classical Latin (as opposed to the Church Latin of the medieval French universities). Montaigne may very well be the last person whose first spoken language was Latin. He gives an account of this seemingly impossible situation in his chapter 'On the Education of Children', where he explains that his father hired a scholar of classical Latin not only to speak Latin to the baby but to provide all family members and servants with enough Latin to interact with the child from day to day. Montaigne knew the language of Cicero before learning that of Chrétien de Troyes. Montaigne was, then, in a sense, the last Roman and an emblematic figure of the French Renaissance, holding together in one person an active social, economic, and civic life (he was mayor of Bordeaux and a *politique* – a political moderate – during the wars of religion) and both an intellectual and imaginative commitment to the texts of Greek and Latin antiquity. In 'Of Vanity', Montaigne recalls that he was familiar with accounts of the Roman capital before he saw the Louvre and that he knew about Lucullus, Metellus, and Scipio before he knew anything about famous Frenchmen. His attachment to the language of Rome was so deep that when, as an adult, years after he had ceased speaking the language of his infancy, he saw his father fall, the first spontaneous expressions of alarm that came to his lips were in Latin. And to complete this life-long identification with Rome, in March 1581 he received the title of 'citizen of Rome' in the form of a *bulla* (certificate with seal), or, as he wrote in French in 'Of Vanity', a *bulle*, which means both 'bull' in the sense of certificate but also 'bubble' – the quintessential representation of vanity itself.

Montaigne's detailed self-description in his *Essays* (1580, with multiple revisions in the 1582 and especially the 1588 and posthumous 1595 edition) had an immediate international resonance. Not only did Montaigne give the world a new genre, the 'essay' (his book was translated into English in 1603 by John Florio as *The essays or Morall, politike and militarie discourses*), but he helped set in motion two trends that became hugely important in the following century: the introspective study of the self, the *moi*, on the one hand, and the dispassionate and often demystifying description of society, on the other. These two trends, most visible in the 17th-century writings known as 'moralist' literature, were not the individual creation of Montaigne nor were they exclusively French. We can see a demystified view of society in Machiavelli earlier and soon after Montaigne in the Spanish writer Gracián, for instance, but more than the analysis of an individual person and of social interaction, the *Essays* show a mind at work, thus drawing the reader in and providing one model for an early-modern personality.

Montaigne's style of writing provided an ideal of naturalness, the kind of book where, as Blaise Pascal wrote later, you expect to find an author but you are surprised and charmed to find a man. Pascal points here to the newness of the essay as a genre. When he says that one does not find an 'author', he means an authoritative figure whose words are received with reverence. Although the *Essays* draw upon many classical sources which, in retrospect, we can call 'essays' (Plutarch's *Moralia* and many texts by Seneca, for instance), Montaigne's decision to say that his book was a collection of 'attempts' signalled this shift in the relation of writer and reader. The author's declared tentativeness about his writing invited readers to be more engaged, perhaps to disagree, and perhaps to find similarities between their own experiences and those of Montaigne. In Montaigne's wake, over the centuries a large number of French writers excelled in this form. Most recently these include Charles Péguy, Paul Valéry, Albert Camus, Paul Nizan, Maurice Blanchot, Roland Barthes, Marguerite Yourcenar, and Pascal Quignard.

Montaigne represents himself as a multi-faceted character. It is, of course, essential to remember that what we have in the *Essays* is not an historical figure pieced together from multiple documents, but rather the first-person character that Montaigne has created through his writing. He insists on the facets of his personality, presenting them often as the opposition between inside and outside, between a Roman and a Frenchman, between 'Montaigne and the mayor of Bordeaux', and between the solitary reader in the tower of his château and the household scene outside his windows. Such awareness of his own complexity permits an ironic detachment leading to surprising juxtapositions: comments on his digestion or his kidney stones appear alongside soaring philosophical speculations, and the activities of simple country people teach as much as the deeds of princes and popes. One of the most memorable examples of this ironic levelling occurs at the end of the chapter 'Of Cannibals', where Montaigne reflected in memorable terms on the valuation of cultural difference and the term 'barbarism'. In a typically sinuous text that starts with a quotation from Plutarch's 'Life of Pyrrhus', turns to the recently discovered American continent and its inhabitants, Atlantis, divination, Stoic philosophy, and many other matters, Montaigne concludes that the 'savages' or 'cannibals' of the New World were not inferior to the French. Montaigne met such an American in Rouen in 1562, and finding his conversation quite intelligent, exclaims, with delicious irony, 'All of that is pretty good. But, of all things, they don't wear breeches!'

For Montaigne, and for many of his contemporaries, the newly discovered peoples of the Americas seemed a possible parallel to the rediscovered ancients. So for his first readers it was probably not so strange to see the *Essays* pass back and forth, as they often did, between Greco-Roman life and that of contemporary Brazil. These new-found peoples offered a glimpse of noble and simple life like that of Homeric heroes or, indeed, a possible pre-Adamite race of humans. The parallel between the distant European past and the American present appears in Montaigne's chapter 'On

Coaches', where he describes the Mexican conception of the major epochs of the world. Like us, he writes, they believe that the world is drawing to its end and is degenerating. In the past there were giants, both figuratively and literally.

## Rabelais's mysterious giants

Two of the world's most memorable giants appear in the books of the physician François Rabelais (c. 1490–1553), who also gave the world two important adjectives: *Gargantuan* and *Pantagruelian*. Rabelais did not invent the two giants Gargantua and Pantagruel – they existed already, as witnessed by an anonymous chapbook of tales that appeared in 1532 under the title *Gargantua: Les grandes et inestimables cronicques du grand et énorme géant Gargantua* – but he turned them into important characters in the literary pantheon, in a series of books published from 1532 to 1552, the first under the anagrammatic pseudonym Alcofrybas Nasier. Successively a Franciscan and then a Benedictine monk, before becoming a physician and making at least three trips to Italy, Rabelais was associated with reformist movements within the Catholic Church and was keenly interested in the new humanist learning and its implications for education and for religion.

The prologue to *Gargantua* sets forth the idea that the book contains secret wisdom and urges readers to suck out the 'substance in the marrow' (*la sustantificque mouelle*). This metaphor of a hidden core is preceded by such sayings as 'the habit does not make the monk' for 'one may be dressed in monastic garb who, inside, is quite other than a monk'. Are Rabelais's books coded messages addressed to Evangelical Christian sympathizers who were deeply sceptical of the Catholic theologians of the universities and of the monastic orders? Are they, on the contrary, the opinions of a rationalistic atheist? Or is the claim to convey a hidden message simply an additional joke accompanying the openly comic material? The debate still rages, but it is clear that for all the carnivalesque goings-on (for instance,

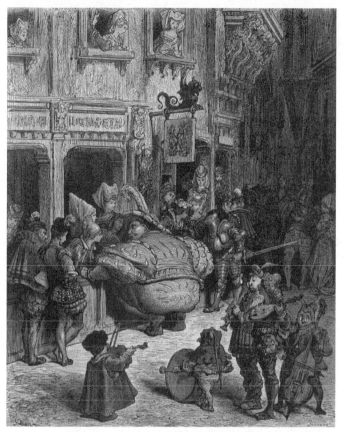

2. **Illustration by Gustave Doré (1854) for Rabelais's *Gargantua* (1534)**

Garguantua, arriving in Paris, relieves himself and drowns several
hundred thousand Parisians) there are major questions about
social institutions raised in the midst of the drinking, urinating,
and brawling. The discontinuous, episodic nature of each book
in the series thrusts the main characters to the foreground as the
major structural elements. Pantagruel is the hero of the first book,

and then his father Gargantua becomes the hero in the second book (a flashback, or 'prequel', to the first), while Pantagruel's companion Panurge is the focus of the third book – Panurge wishes to marry but fears being cuckolded and tries a variety of ways to predict his fate in marriage.

As we look backwards from our modern vantage point towards Rabelais's heroes, it is striking to note the quite relaxed integration of popular and learned cultures, of grossly physical with highly erudite and spiritual questions – the eating and drinking in *Gargantua* is explicitly connected with Plato's *Symposium*. Although some works of the following century strive to maintain this mix of character, subject, and tone (for example, Charles Sorel's *Histoire comique de Francion*, 1623–33, quite clearly inspired by Rabelais), for the most part the enormous physicality and appetite of Gargantua and Pantagruel and their humour are absent from the high-culture novels, comedies, and tragedies of the 17th century. In terms of the century-long effort to assimilate the humanistic culture of antiquity into a French, as opposed to an Italian or Italianate, model, Rabelais clearly succeeded in giving the French hugely learned and subtle protagonists deeply rooted in French geography, customs, and language.

## The French sonnet

The lure of Italian sophistication and the countervailing pull backwards towards French simplicity appear as themes in Renaissance lyric, particularly in such works as Joachim du Bellay's *The Regrets* (1558), in which the first-person poet-character compares life in Rome to his memories of home. Du Bellay's importance for shaping modern French literature goes beyond his many successes in lyric, for he was also the author of the manifesto of his innovative poetic group, the Pléiade, a group of seven poets formed in the late 1540s that included Pierre de Ronsard. This manifesto, the *Defense and Illustration of the French Language* (*la Défense et Illustration de la Langue*

*Française*, 1649) argued for enriching the vocabulary of French and building its cultural repertory to make it equal to Italian and the languages of antiquity. The *Defense* appeared ten years after the royal ordinance of Villers-Cotterêts by which François I made the vernacular the language of official documents (replacing Latin). Thus the *Defense* furthers the promotion of French linguistic nationalism that the King had begun, and it also assigns to the professional poet a role that is not limited to singing the praises of kings and military heroes. Not only does the *Defense* make it clear that poetry – in the broad sense, not only lyric, but also epic, comedy, and tragedy – is a discipline, rather than a sudden inspiration or simply the result of a certain temperament, but also that the poet's work as word-maker and language-builder assigns to him a broad and varied cultural mandate. Du Bellay proposed various ways of creating and importing words into French, but he particularly promoted the idea – the doctrine of imitation – that French writers should make literary equivalents of ancient works rather than simple translations. In other words, that France should have French epics, French lyrics, and so forth, rather than simply import the works of others. Du Bellay's polemical work serves as a document of the serious ambitions of poets in the period, but today we may also see it as an early expression of France's struggle to maintain its own identity in the face of whatever other culture is the dominant global model, whether it be that of Renaissance Rome or of today's Hollywood.

Following such models as Ovid, Horace, and Catullus, each of the major writers in verse shaped for himself or herself a distinct character or persona in the ballads, rondeaux, poetic epistles, elegies, epitaphs, blazons (verse descriptions, particularly of parts of the female body), complaints, epigrams, and odes that appeared abundantly in the 16th century. Many of the most important works took the form of long sequences of ten-verse (the *dizain*) or fourteen-verse (the sonnet) units. The *dizain* is the unit that Maurice Scève, one of the poets of Lyon (who include also Pernette du Guillet and 'Louise Labé' – the latter may in fact be simply a fictitious identity under which a collective of male poets published their works), used for his long hermetic love poem, *Délie, object de plus haulte vertu* (*Délie, object of the highest virtue*, 1544), a sequence of 449 *dizains*. The sonnet, on the other hand, has had more durable success, and the form itself testifies to the impact of Italian literature. Clément Marot, the first great poet of the 16th century, like Rabelais a protégé of Marguerite de Navarre, brought the Petrarchan sonnet to France in the 1530s.

It was in the 1550s, though, that the sonnet triumphed in the works of the Pléiade poets, each of whom gives a different tonality to the form in connection with the different persona the poet wished to create. Pierre Ronsard, for instance, variously portrays the character 'Ronsard' as suffering horribly from love or as the triumphant poet whose transcendent verbal gifts will be able to confer immortality upon the woman who grants her favours. Take, for instance, the well-known sonnet from the *Second Book of Sonnets for Hélène* that begins:

French Literature

> *Quand vous serez bien vieille, au soir à la chandelle,*
> *Assise auprès du feu, dévidant et filant,*
> *Direz chantant mes vers, en vous émerveillant:*
> *'Ronsard me célébrait du temps que j'étais belle'.*

[When you will be very old, during candle-lit evenings, / Sitting next to the fire, carding and spinning, / You will say, singing my verses with amazement, / 'Ronsard sang my praises when I was beautiful'.]

The poet cleverly inserts himself into the text, not by presenting himself here in the first person but rather by having a character speak about him as if he were a prodigy. 'Ronsard' becomes a character for retrospective admiration in this text which is a variation on the ancient *carpe diem*. As the 'Prince of Poets', Ronsard was not shy about celebrating his own talent, and, implicitly, the supreme position of the poet in society. In his 'Response to Insults and Calumnies', he wrote of his success in reviving ancient poetry and asserts to his detractors, 'You cannot deny it, since from my plenitude / You are all filled, I am the centre of your study, / You have all come from the grandeur of me' (*Tu ne le peux nier, car de ma plenitude / Vous estes tous remplis, je suis seul vostre estude, / Vous estes tous yssus de la grandeur de moy*).

## An exemplary sonnet-sequence: du Bellay's *The Regrets*

Let us return to Ronsard's companion du Bellay, whose *The Regrets*, often considered his greatest work, is particularly useful for capturing the emulation, enthusiasm, and anxiety that French writers felt when facing the more advanced culture of Italy. The poet, as first-person character of his own disillusioning adventures in the capital of Roman antiquity, highlights national and linguistic identity, promoting the idea of a humble, frank-speaking native son of the Loire valley adrift in the pomp and decadence of the papal court. But *The Regrets* is also a book that advances the idea of a poetry based on accidental encounter – 'Following the various incidents of this place, / Whether they are good or bad, I write at random' (*Mais, suivant de ce lieu les accidents divers, / Soit de bien, soit de mal, j'escris à l'adventure*). While this claim is literally unsustainable in the context of a sequence written in the dauntingly artful and constraining form of the sonnet, it situates the poetic 'I' as a humble observer of the contemporary world. This is a poetic persona that, even if it is somewhat rooted in Villon and Rutebeuf, gains momentum much later in the French tradition, with Baudelaire and the Surrealists, and even appears to prefigure James Joyce, insofar as du Bellay, while exploring the city, tries on a comparison to ancient poets and epic heroes, most strikingly Ulysses.

*The Regrets* are an open-ended, varied work with multiple tones – satiric, elegiac, conversational, descriptive, and at times stirringly celebratory ('France, mother of arts, of arms, and of laws', *France, mère des arts, des armes et des lois* – a striking reversal of his

Heureux qui, comme Ulysse, a fait un beau voyage,

Ou comme cestuy-là qui conquit la toison,

Et puis est retourné, plein d'usage et raison,

Vivre entre ses parents le reste de son aage!

Quand revoiray-je, helas, de mon petit village

Fumer la cheminee: et en quelle saison

Revoiray-je le clos de ma pauvre maison,

Qui m'est une province, et beaucoup davantage?

Plus me plaist le séjour qu'ont basty mes ayeux,

Que des palais Romains le front audacieux:

Plus que le marbre dur me plaist l'ardoise fine,

Plus mon Loyre Gaulois, que le Tybre Latin,

Plus mon petit Lyré, que le mont Palatin,

Et plus que l'air marin la doulceur Angevine.

Joachim du Bellay, from Les Regrets

Happy the man who, like Ulysses, has travelled well, or like that man who conquered the fleece, and has then returned, full of experience and wisdom, to live among his kinsfolk the rest of his life.

When, alas, will I again see smoke rising from the chimney of my little village and in what season will I see the enclosed field of my poor house, which to me is a province and much more still?

> The home my ancestors built pleases me more than the grandiose facades of Roman palaces, fine slate pleases me more than hard marble,
>
> My Gallic Loire more than the Latin Tiber, my little Liré more than the Palatine hill, and more than sea air, the sweetness of Anjou.
>
> Translated by Richard Helgerson

nation's relation to Rome). Its most direct successor in modern French literature may be Baudelaire's post-Romantic *Fleurs du mal*. It was only a few years after *The Regrets* that the wars of religion between varying factions of Protestants and Catholics (1562–98) profoundly changed French culture and set the stage for the more highly structured and often less personal literature of the 17th century.

# Chapter 3

# Society and its demands

## A precarious peace and the new civility

Politeness, moderation, discretion, self-censorship, irony, and a great attention to the formal rituals of civil and religious life are the hallmarks of 17th-century France. Looking back from today, it is tempting to speak of a very repressed and repressive society. Seen from the point of view of those who had lived through the ferocious civil and religious wars of the late 16th century, the peace and stability, and a modicum of religious tolerance, were no doubt welcome. The 1594 coronation of the first Bourbon monarch, Henri IV, brought peace to France through compromise. Henri, son of the intransigent Protestant Jeanne d'Albret, converted to Catholicism, while the militant Catholic League, bane of the late Valois monarchs (accused of being too willing to coexist with the Huguenots), put down their arms.

In 1598, Henri proclaimed the Edict of Nantes, granting Protestants the right to worship. Under Henri IV and his son and successor Louis XIII, Paris grew rapidly in size and became the habitual home of the royal court. Both the nobility and a prosperous middle class flocked to the new neighbourhoods – especially to the Marais (named from the reclaimed swamp on which it was built) on the right bank of the Seine slightly upriver from the Louvre. The upper classes of

French society became more urban and more urbane, though not without effort. Many books, plays, and letters attest to the earnest discussions of how to achieve the proper skill in witty conversation, letter-writing, and dress. This effort to fit in and to avoid giving offence, or at least to channel violence into inventive verbal forms, hints that physical aggression was lurking just under the surface. Henri IV was assassinated in 1610, as his predecessor Henri III had been in 1589. Repeated edicts failed to prevent duels – there were as many as four hundred a year under Henri IV.

Everyone was aware of the precarious peace, and throughout France there was an effort to promote ways of interacting politely and to avoid setting off a new round of hostility. In this climate flourished a literature that promoted an ideal of moderation, discretion, and even concealment, yet was fascinated by excess, by the exceptional, and by the superlative. It is as if the polite and decorous 17th-century French still dreamed of the martyrdom and the transgressive heroism of the preceding century and also reflected on the difficulty of determining a set of norms. There was great emphasis on avoiding highly visible partisanship and zealotry, and on being a reasonable person, an amusing, sensitive, and accommodating companion – in short, an *honnête homme*. This term is not easily translated, and it is important to note right away that it does not mean 'honest man' in the sense of someone who speaks with sincerity and complete frankness. The *honnête homme* is someone who 'fits in', who is not notably eccentric. On the other hand, 17th-century readers and authors were captivated by the stories of protagonists who go far beyond the norm, who do not 'fit in' at all and who are excessive in word and deed.

## Molière's comedy of character

As the ideal of the polite society reached its peak, theatre showed that politeness and heroism were an uneasy fit. Take Molière's

**3. Chateau of Vaux-le-Vicomte, designed by Louis Le Vau, in an engraving by Perelle (1660)**

comic hero Alceste in *The Misanthrope* (1666, called in French *Le Misanthrope, ou l'Atrabilaire amoureux*). The full title refers to the medical doctrine that character was based on substances in the blood, the 'humours'. Hence, Alceste is a man with too much black bile who is in love. The role of Alceste, performed by the playwright himself in the first production, was certainly played for laughs. Molière was known for his comic stagecraft, and there is much to laugh about. The hero, who insists that one should speak one's mind fearlessly in all matters, falls in love with a woman who is his complete opposite, a flirtatious young widow. Célimène carefully cultivates a number of suitors by making each think that he is the exclusive object of her affection. Alceste also refuses to conform to many ordinary social norms. He will not condescend to flatter the judge in an important legal matter involving his entire fortune, and he even refuses to utter the usual formulas of polite approval when an amateur poet shows him a sonnet. He recognizes that he is a misfit in the court where an important quality is the gift to 'hide what is in one's heart' (as Alceste's friend Philinte says). For his sincerity, Alceste faces three risks: losing Célimène's love, losing his fortune, and losing his life or his reputation in a duel. These risks seem to be of quite unequal importance, and it is probably Molière's comic intent to show the bizarre disproportion between various gestures of frankness and their results. The possible duel, a serious matter and reflective of the brittle civility that could pass in minutes from witty repartee to drawn swords, leads to the intervention of the *Maréchaux de France*, a high tribunal charged with settling conflicts of honour and thus avoiding bloodshed. Despite Alceste's repeated proclamations that he will not conform to society and that he will eventually run away to live in solitude, he seems to need society – if for no other reason than for the pleasure of his own indignation. In this respect, he differs from such other contemporary outsiders as the wolf in Jean de La Fontaine's fable, 'The Wolf and the Dog' (*Le Loup et le chien*, in *Fables*, 1668). The wolf, despite the many material advantages that the dog enjoys in captivity, really prefers to remain entirely outside society. The misanthrope, on the other hand, seems only to be able to exist within proximity to those he distains.

It is tempting to think that Alceste is entirely ridiculous, an unstable individual with too much bile, no social skills, and no sense of proportion. Yet the play dispels that view by having the other characters in *Le Misanthrope* admire Alceste and vie for his friendship, love, and approval. Some of these characters may themselves be lacking in judgement, like Oronte, author of the sonnet, but others, like Alceste's friend Philinte and Célimène's cousin Éliante appear to be good judges of character. Philinte is a fine example of the 17th-century *honnête homme*: he never advances any particular achievement of his own (La Rochefoucauld said just this in his 1664 *Maxims*: 'The true *honnête homme* is the one who does not attach his pride to anything in particular'), he views human imperfections with tolerance and detachment, saying that 'there is no greater madness than to try to set the world straight'. Alceste describes Philinte as phlegmatic (another imbalance of the humours),

**4. Engraving by François Chauveau (1668) for La Fontaine's fable *Le Loup et le chien***

meaning that he is too placid. And this may be a key to Alceste's attractiveness for those around him, men and women alike: they are spellbound by his vigorous, unbending candour, reflected in his physical agitation: he seems to be constantly in motion, with the others running after him. They may well find it refreshing to see someone free of the self-consciousness and dissimulation that is their daily lot.

## Corneille's outsized heroes

This ambivalence about heroism in the *Misanthrope* may be a comic example, but it is not isolated. The pattern we see there, of a society that is spellbound, yet appalled, by the energetic, dissenting hero, appears in other, more serious forms. We can see that the 17th-century insistence on politeness – the expectation of conformity to what fits the situation (in French, *convenance* or *bienséance*) – is based on the fear that people who stand out and who say heroically what they think could so easily cross over into the explosive violence of the still-recent civil wars. In *Horace* (1640), based on Livy's account of the ancient combat between the three Roman champions, the Horatii, and the three champions of the nearby city of Alba Longa, the Curiatii, Corneille presents the moral dilemma of one of the three Romans, who must fight his best friend and brother-in-law, Curiace. The fight will be limited to three warriors from each city, in the interest of a quick and relatively bloodless decision about political dominance. Unlike the reluctant Curiace, Horace claims to be so completely focused on his duty that from the moment when he learns the identity of his adversary he no longer 'knows' Curiace: 'Alba named you, I know you no more'. So far, this may be no more than a case of doing what it takes in the line of duty – a bit cold-hearted, perhaps, and not very polite, but the way to victory. Indeed, Horace does win for the Roman side, for he is the last man standing of the six.

However, it is at this point, the moment of the hero's return from the battlefield, that Horace's attitude towards his own heroism crosses the line into civil violence. Horace's sister Camille was Curiace's lover, and she does not greet him with the respect that he demands, saying to her 'render [the honour] that you owe to the fortune of my victory'. He is, to say the least, unfeeling, focused entirely on his brilliant achievement and, as he said earlier, unwilling to recognize any personal attachment or identity in this state of war. But this extremism, or even fanaticism, is matched by his sister's – it runs in the family, apparently – for instead of yielding and keeping silent, she insults him and escalates the verbal combat to the point of cursing the Rome that Horace claims to incarnate. She calls down the fire of heaven on the city. The altercation between Camille and her brother is the most violent part of the play as it appears on stage, for the sword fight between Albans and Romans takes place off stage, as does almost all physical violence in French drama after the 1630s.

And this second encounter ends badly for Horace. He becomes so enraged that he kills his sister. For what he then calls 'an act of justice', he is put on trial. The play culminates, then, in a full act devoted to the incompatibility between unflinching, unfeeling, Horatian-style heroism and the requirements of a society of laws, individual identities and duties, and political hierarchy. In the civil society that is depicted in Corneille's version of Rome, the purely masculine virtues required in war cannot be allowed to run unchecked. As Horace's chief accuser, Valère, points out, by shedding his sister's blood, Horace has not only killed an unarmed woman but a Roman citizen. The violence that was tolerable when it took place outside the city and aimed itself against non-Romans has now entered the city itself to threaten all. The most general paradox that Corneille displays here is that while the peaceful civil order is based on fratricide (Rome's war against its kindred city Alba, like Horace's murder of his sister, is set in the perspective of Rome's legendary founding by Romulus, killer of his brother Remus), such violence should never be rekindled.

Though important for any consideration of heroism, the general paradox of the warrior's return to the city is less original than the insight into Horace's own experience of this status that Corneille subtly conveys. Generations of audiences and readers have generally found Horace to be much less appealing a character than his opponent Curiace, but the play suggests a terrible suffering within the hero. The price of his victory has been the sacrifice of all feeling, all perception that is not directly oriented towards slaying the designated enemy. And that sacrifice is directed at a single moment, after which, inevitably, the hero begins to decline into an ordinary life that is forever closed to him. Horace asks to be executed, claiming that 'Death alone today can preserve my glory / And it should have come at the moment of my triumph'. At the end of *Horace*, just as at the end of *The Misanthrope*, the audience is left to puzzle over how such an outsized, unyielding protagonist can fit back into the ordinary social world.

# The decline of the hero

Heroes, in other words, are useful to have around at certain moments, but fit awkwardly into the social framework over the long haul. They are not necessarily even 'good' by prevailing moral standards. La Rochefoucauld wrote memorably that 'There are heroes of evil as well as of good'; we need only think of two of Corneille's other protagonists, both heroic and monstrous – Medea in his first tragedy *Médée* (1635) and Cleopatra in *Rodogune, princesse des Parthes* (1644) – or of Racine's later depiction of the Emperor Nero in *Britannicus* (1669). As literary theorists tried to square the heritage of ancient tragedy with Christian, modern values, there was considerable unease at placing characters capable of extreme acts, good and bad, in the position of 'hero'. Corneille's younger rival Jean Racine paraphrased Aristotle's dictum in the *Poetics* on tragic heroes, saying that they should have 'a middling goodness, that is, a virtue susceptible to weakness'. Racine worked to create characters with this middling goodness, or *bonté médiocre*. Avoiding the spectacular qualities and acts of such Corneille protagonists as Horace, Chimène in *Le Cid*, and Auguste in *Cinna*, Racine in most of his tragedies depicted protagonists who are quite middling, even 'mediocre' in the modern sense. They are people like ourselves, or like the version of ourselves we see on day-time television, but in magnificent verse. Such are the protagonists of *Phèdre*, in which the eponymous protagonist is an unfortunate woman who has fallen in love with her adolescent stepson – she considers herself a monster, but this is the 'monster' next door, who, once rebuffed, acquiesces to a plan to accuse Hippolyte of raping her.

We can see why it has been said that Racine turned tragedy into bourgeois melodrama. In his *Andromaque* (1668), a tragedy which takes its title from Andromache, the widow of the Trojan hero Hector, now become the slave of Achilles' son Pyrrhus, Racine illustrates this concept of the protagonist of middling goodness with such thoroughness that one might even be tempted to say with Karl Marx that 'history repeats itself, the first time as tragedy, the second as farce'. The main characters of this play belong – with the possible exception of Andromaque herself – to a post-heroic generation. Their parents were the great Homeric heroes and heroines of the *Iliad*, Agamemnon, Helen, Menelaus, Achilles, and yet the new generation of Hermione, Orestes, and even (though to a less marked extent) Pyrrhus is obsessed with a desire to live up to and compete with its forebears. Hermione recalls that her mother was so beautiful that the Trojan war was fought to bring her back to Greece, yet she cannot even get Pyrrhus to honour his promise of marriage to her. Orestes dithers irresolutely over his unrequited love for Hermione, failing to carry out his ambassadorial mission, which is to find and slay Hector's son Astyanax to eliminate all trace of the royal family of Troy. Pyrrhus himself is described as the 'son and rival of Achilles'. But while their parents shook the world with epic battles, this group ends up with a sordid palace intrigue of murder and suicide.

Yet despite the clear difference between the larger-than-life protagonists of Corneille and even Molière and Racine's self-consciously mediocre characters, there is a remarkable similarity with regard to the ambivalent theme of heroism. The reason that the protagonists of *Andromaque* arrive at their dreadful end is that they tried to stage heroic feats for which they did not have the ability and which, in any event (and this is the most striking parallel with the historical situation of 17th-century France) belonged to the past and should have been left in the past. In *Andromaque*, just as in *Horace*, the moment in which it was useful to act as violent military heroes has gone by, and the protagonists would have been well advised to adopt the skills of peacetime. A certain amount of heroism is admirable, as Molière's *honnête homme* Philinte might have said, but there is a time and place for everything.

These major dramatic works give us some sense of the continuity in the way civility, conformity to circumstance, and politeness were proposed as ideals, even when they were projected back into the French version of Greco-Roman antiquity. But we should now recall the social circumstances that gave these ideals such weight, and even urgency. The transition from the religious wars of the 16th century to the more stable, and even more bureaucratic, regime of the Bourbon monarchs was not at all easy. The assassination of Henri IV was a great blow; the subsequent regency of Marie de Médicis ended with a *coup d'état* staged by her son, King Louis XIII, whose long-serving prime minister, Cardinal Richelieu, executed, imprisoned, or exiled members of the 'devout party' which derived in large part from the Catholic League that had been such a challenge to the last Valois and to Henri IV before his conversion. But outright civil war returned at mid-century during the tumultuous and complicated time known as the 'Fronde' ('slingshot' in French), which lasted from 1648 to 1653, and set troops loyal to the regent Queen Anne of Austria against a fluctuating alliance of nobility and *parlementaires* (members of the Paris legislative court).

This confrontation ended, after devastating large parts of the country, by reaffirming the monarchy. The ambivalence towards aristocratic, independent heroism – newly illustrated by the rebellion or treason of the Prince de Condé and of the King's uncle Gaston d'Orléans who allied themselves with Spain against the Queen – could only be reinforced by this catastrophic and wasteful adventure, which left a deep impression on the young Louis XIV, only ten years old when the Fronde began. In the decisive steps taken to further centralize power and to remove any remaining independence from the upper aristocracy, Louis made conformity – outward conformity, at least – a central value of French culture of the second half of the century. This certainly is one of the reasons why the status of the hero as it appears in the three major dramatists shows a significant downward trajectory from Corneille to Racine, even though all three show heroism as leading to conflict.

Another reason for the change in the status of the hero may be the rise in influence, towards mid-century, of a disenchanted worldview associated with the religious movement known as Jansenism, centred on the convent of Port-Royal, and influential with many leading writers of the 'moralist' tendency, such as Blaise Pascal and François de La Rochefoucauld. This movement was not simply about advocating austere morality (though some, like Pascal, were quite ascetic), but rather in large part it consisted of giving a pessimistic view of human society and its motives, and aimed at a dispassionate analysis of relationships. It saw mankind as anything but heroic.

In the second half of the century, a different type of protagonist emerged, in keeping with the intensification of court and

### Salons and the rise of literary women

The term 'salon' is now used somewhat anachronistically (the term itself became prominent only in the 18th century) to describe the private meeting places where women received guests in the 17th century – major contemporary terms for such places were *ruelle*, *alcôve*, or *réduit*, meaning the narrow space between a bed and the nearby wall in which guests might stand or sit to converse with the hostess, who remained recumbent. Two such *salons* stand out: the *Chambre bleue* of the Marquise de Rambouillet and the *samedis* (Saturdays) of Madeleine de Scudéry. These cultivated women controlled the space into which they invited distinguished male as well as female guests, making the *salons* women-centred conversational places in sharp distinction to the taverns in which male writers might meet on their own. The values promoted in this environment included freedom from arranged marriages and friendship between women and men. Detractors of women such as Boileau called them *précieuses*, a term Molière popularized in his *Précieuses ridicules* (1659) and *L'École des femmes* (*The School for Wives*, 1662).

urban life in proximity to the court, with the domestication of the aristocracy, and with moralist disenchantment. This new protagonist is typical of a trend – or of a number of converging trends – in which there is an 'inward turn' of literature, a turn towards 'literature of psychological analysis', a social and cultural movement called *préciosité*, and the rise of social spaces, the *salons*, organized by women.

## The novel of courtly manners

In this context, emphasis shifts to a new conception of the hero, or rather of the protagonist (since the term 'hero' was generally not used for non-military distinction): the person who exemplified exquisite refinement in friendship and love and was capable of exceptional fidelity to ideals. No one exemplifies this type of protagonist better than the central figure of Marie-Madeleine de Lafayette's brief novel, *La Princesse de Clèves* (published anonymously, 1678). This work, often praised as one of the first 'psychological novels' or 'novels of analysis', is set in the Valois court of the previous century. Arriving at Paris with her widowed mother at age 16, the protagonist, an innocent young woman, receives from her mother three basic instructions about the world she is about to enter. The first is to distrust appearances: what seems to be is almost never the case. The second, somewhat contradictory, lesson is to learn from listening to stories about the wretched experiences of other men and women at the court. And the third lesson is that for a woman, the only way to happiness consists of loving her husband and being loved by him in return – in short, to be completely different from other women, typified by those whose tales she hears and who are engaged in multiple, unhappy, adulterous love affairs. From the very start of her story, then, the heroine aims both to understand and to be different from other women, and to find that elusive happiness that is said to be available only to the happily married woman.

As the wife of the perfectly honourable Prince de Clèves, the young woman soon meets the highly desirable Duc de Nemours, whose reputation as a lover is universal. The love affair that follows is one in which the Princess and the Duke are alone on only two occasions, never touch, and are never publicly known to have feelings for one another. Despite the constant surveillance, intense curiosity, and gossip of the court, the story of the Princess's discovery of love and of her own nature is known to no one except, in part, to the Princess, her husband, her mother, and the Duke himself. It is tempting to say that it is a story in which nothing happens, yet, adjusting the scale of perception, we can see how Lafayette has moved events inward, into the minds and feelings of her characters, where life-and-death struggles occur and virtue is pitted against betrayal. Tiny, almost imperceptible, signals allow the characters to communicate with one another. For instance, the Duke, wishing to show his affection for the Princess in a way that could never be understood by anyone except herself, identifies himself at a tournament by wearing yellow and black. Everyone wonders why, since these colours had no apparent connection to him. The Princess, however, immediately understands that it is a favour to her, for one day at a conversation at which the Duke was present, she had said that she liked yellow but could not wear it because she was blonde. On another occasion, the Princess did not go to a ball, claiming to be ill (though she appeared to be in radiant good health). This is another of those secret signals, since the Princess has heard it reported that the Duke said that there was no greater suffering for a lover than to know that his mistress was at a ball that he himself was not able to attend.

The heroism of the battlefield, the exotic locations, the very visible hostilities that pit the protagonists against one another in tragedy, epic, and the huge romance novels of earlier in the century, have here been replaced by the subtle decoding of glances, details of dress, and presence or absence at balls and other social gatherings. But what gives the Princess a status equivalent to the protagonists of these other texts is her problematic uniqueness. With her mother's initial guidance, the Princess formed and then executed a heroic project: to be different from all other women. Some of this distinction is visible to a few of the members of the court. One of the queens says that the Princess is the only woman who tells her husband everything. In fact, the Princess confesses privately to her husband that she loves someone else, while keeping that man's name secret and promising never to be unfaithful – this avowal was one of the most shocking and controversial aspects of the novel when it appeared. But the Duke himself is the only person in the novel who knows the full extent of her heroic resolve. After her husband's death (of a broken heart, because he has improperly decoded a set of appearances and wrongly believes his wife to be unfaithful – this is a novel in which misinterpretation is lethal), in a brief conversation, the Princess admits to her lover that their passion is mutual, but that she will never marry him. She intends, as she tells him, to act according to a duty that 'only exists in my imagination' not to marry the man who was, indirectly and unwittingly, the cause of her husband's death. Throughout the novel, and particularly in its conclusion, the Princess is described as being unparalleled, unique, and exceptional. The last sentence of the novel ends: 'her life, which was rather short, left examples of inimitable virtue'.

With *The Princess of Clèves*, Lafayette showed the cost of being exceptional and not following the prevailing model of conduct – in this, the story fits the model we saw earlier in tragedy and comedy – but she also shows how changes in French culture and in the status of women modified the standard for what is worthy of attention and for what constitutes exceptional achievement. For 17th-century feminists, a woman's decision to be independent, not to remarry, and to form her own ideal of conduct constituted a story at least as interesting as that of a male military hero. Starting with her mother's lesson that a happy marriage was the only worthy goal for a woman, the Princess ended with a very different achievement.

# Chapter 4
# Nature and its possibilities

## The problem of 'nature'

Given the intense focus on society and its norms that characterized the 17th century, it is perhaps not surprising that the 18th century should react in part against this exclusive focus and shift the discussion to the question of nature. The opposition between nature and culture (or between *physis* and *nomos*) is very ancient, but it took on a new vitality in the 18th century. 17th-century French thought, particularly in literary circles, was not kind to nature. It seemed clear that the world was defective and that religion and art had the mission of correcting things or, at the very least, of filtering out the naturally occurring errors. Left to himself – to his temperament, since that was determined by the imbalance in his humours – Molière's Alceste would be miserable and unfit for society. His friends try to counterbalance that tendency by teaching him manners. In a more serious vein, Pascal taught that mankind's nature had been fundamentally altered by Original Sin, so that what we call 'natural' is only a perverse illusion – Pascal is here very close to Thomas Hobbes, a long-time resident of Paris, who had nothing good to say about the 'state of nature'. Finally, by the literary doctrine of *vraisemblance*, the French Academy and others taught that dramatists should not portray what happens in the ordinary course of things but rather what should happen, if the world were not imperfect. In short, any 17th-century writer who used the term 'nature' in a positive way meant something that was far removed from the world of experience. Writers often praised the 'natural' manner of speaking, only to point out that such a style could only be achieved by careful imitation of the best models; in other words, *le naturel* was the best form of artifice. As for the relatively modern notion that one could go 'into nature' (*dans la nature*) by leaving the city, such a sense of a privileged unspoiled space would have appeared complete nonsense to the subjects of Louis XIV.

This uniformly dismissive view of nature began to change in the 18th century. Society was still at the forefront of intellectual and literary discussions, but now nature became a component of that discussion in a much more varied and less predictable way. Indeed, for the Enlightenment, Nature – both human nature and the wild forces of the earth – was, broadly speaking, at the core of most important questions. Was nature good but somehow concealed and distorted by social institutions and habits? Or was nature indifferent, or even hostile, to mankind, and should people therefore cease to appeal to nature as the source of concepts of 'good' and 'rights'? Was nature composed of spirit and matter, or was nature purely material and fully available to us through sensations? Nature no longer seemed inaccessible to experience. The earlier, more optimistic views of Montaigne and Rabelais now returned in a very much amplified and better documented way. While Montaigne found much to praise (and many things that shocked him) in what he learned of the indigenous Americans, exploration, commerce, and colonialism brought much more information about life outside of Europe. It was not simply that the peoples of Brazil or of the South Pacific islands were closer to 'nature' (in the sense that their settlements were smaller and seemed less urban and technologically advanced), but also that the multitude of customs and fundamental laws, things that seem entirely self-evident, was found to be so different from one culture to another that what French people took for granted as 'nature' no longer seemed secure. The quest to discover, or rediscover, nature and to refound society on the basis of this surer knowledge was perhaps the major theme of the Enlightenment, *l'âge des Lumières*.

These issues are not always raised with the intention to challenge tradition, since, after all, many French writers argued in favour of the established order. At first glance, the plays and novels of Pierre de Marivaux (1688–1763) appear to have little to do with 'nature'. His comedies of manners are known for their highly artful banter, so characteristic of his style that it gave us the word *marivaudage* for witty, flirtatious dialogue. Yet when we consider the enthusiastic audience for his plays, for instance *The Game of Love and Chance* (*Le Jeu de l'amour et du hasard*, 1730), we can see that Marivaux and his contemporaries were keenly aware of the possible divergence between nature and culture within a social system based on what we would call 'class' and what was then called 'condition'. A young woman, wishing to learn the true personality of the young man to whom her father has arranged to marry her, disguises herself as her maid. Little does she know that the young man has made the same exchange of identity with his valet and for the same purpose. Two couples form, in both cases assembling a man and a woman of the same real, but not apparent, condition – the disguised upper-class characters fall in love with each other.

This was a reassuringly conservative conclusion for Marivaux and his public, and conveyed the message that rank in society is not a superficial convention (as some of the more daring passages of Pascal's *Pensées* a hundred years earlier seemed to suggest) but rather has deeper roots, whether purely inherited or based on long cultivation. But the very fact that the subject of an entire play could be made out of this experiment – and in fact, not only one play, for similar issues appear throughout Marivaux's work – implies that the fear of a misalignment between one's natural characteristics and one's condition was quite present in the first half of the 18th century. Plays highlighting such possible social misalignment continued to have great success in the following years, as Beaumarchais's *The Barber of Seville* (*Le Barbier de Séville*, 1775) shows. It is at least partly in order to accommodate the more serious and less conservative development of these social thematics that French theatre created new genres in the course of the century, including 'tearful comedy' (*la comédie larmoyante*) and the 'drama' (*le drame*).

## Enlightenment and the *philosophes*

While Marivaux was entertaining spectators by showing that, in the end, the social system was secure, a group that he particularly scorned, the *philosophes*, was raising serious questions about birth, rank, and the 'natural' basis of civilization. Jean-Jacques Rousseau (1712–78) published his *Discourse on the Origins of Inequality* (*Discours sur l'origine et les fondements de l'inégalité parmi les hommes*, 1755), arguing that humankind had been happy in the original state of nature prior to the institution of private property, laws, and the social superstructure that maintains inequality. Denis Diderot (1713–84) and Jean le Rond d'Alembert (1717–83) organized the *Encyclopédie* (1751–72, most of it published clandestinely), to which they and approximately 150 other writers contributed anonymous articles. The *philosophes*, a heterogeneous group rent by quarrels, were less 'philosophers' in the modern sense, or even in the sense that Descartes was a philosopher, than they were public intellectuals committed to undoing superstition and ignorance and advocating pragmatic or technocratic solutions to problems of human life in society. Much of their work consisted of promoting a deeper and demystified understanding of the material world as it can be perceived through the senses. This aspect can be seen in Diderot's *On the Interpretation of Nature* (1753–4) concerning sense perceptions, but the encyclopedists also promoted contractual monarchy based on natural law and free enterprise. Their theory of knowledge is empiricist and rationalist and, accordingly, their treatment of knowledge about God is squarely within philosophy rather than within a revealed religion.

One of the best examples of the efforts of the *philosophes* to reach a wide audience through entertaining yet didactic works is Voltaire's *Candide*, a *conte philosophique* (*philosophical tale*) published anonymously in 1759. The immediate target of this satirical tale is Gottfried Leibniz's *Essais de théodicée* (1710), in which the philsopher argued that God has created the best of all possible worlds, the 'optimal' world. In such a system, there is no objective evil. It was to describe Leibniz's position that the term '*optimisme*' entered the French language in 1737. The full title of Voltaire's tale is *Candide ou l'optimisme, traduit de l'allemand de M. le Docteur Ralph* [...]. The well-known story (the basis of the 1956 operetta *Candide* with score by Leonard Bernstein) follows the adventures of Candide, a German from Westphalia who was educated in his youth by Dr Pangloss (the Greek roots suggesting that he can speak about anything, probably a dig at Leibniz's prolific polymathic output) who teaches a teleological optimism: everything was created providentially for the best and could not be otherwise. Pangloss's assertions immediately appear absurd to the reader but not to Candide:

> everything being made for an end, all is necessarily for the best end. Consider that noses were made to wear spectacles: therefore we have spectacles. Legs were clearly made to be in hose, and we have hose.

As a literary creation, Candide is a highly successful character in both common meanings of the term: as a narrative 'person' and as the possessor of a certain 'character' (or personality trait) taken to its extreme. Voltaire describes him at the outset by saying 'He had reasonably good judgment along with complete simplicity; that's why, I think, they called him Candide' (*Il avait le jugement assez droit, avec l'esprit le plus simple; c'est, je crois, pour cette raison qu'on le nommait Candide*). For Voltaire's satire of Leibnizian optimism and of all those who cling to ideologies in order to avoid facing unpleasant realities, it is important that the personage we follow around the globe be a mixture of perceptiveness and exceptional persistence within the rigid doctrine that Pangloss taught. Thus Voltaire was able to continue accumulating examples of natural horror (the Lisbon earthquake of 1755), Roman Catholic hypocrisy and intolerance (the *autodafé* in which the Portuguese priests burned three men to prevent further earthquakes; the grand inquisitor's sexual activities; the Jesuit kingdom in Paraguay), the murderous cruelty of European kingdoms and the empire, the mutilations of African slaves in Surinam, and various examples of venality and corruption, while Candide only very slowly gives up his reassuring Panglossian certitude that there must be a good reason for all this. By the time he sees the slave whose leg has been amputated as punishment for attempting to escape and whose hand has been cut off to get it out of the way of the sugar grinder, Candide does, however, exclaim 'Oh Pangloss!...you did not know of this abomination. That's it – I will have to renounce your optimism.' When asked at this point what 'optimism' is, Candide replies, 'It's the mania of claiming that everything is all right when you are suffering' (*c'est la rage de soutenir que tout est bien quand on est mal*). If Leibniz had been Voltaire's only target, and if he had not so perfectly matched his hero to the road show of horrors to produce such comic dissonance, *Candide* would not have survived in the popular imagination. But what Voltaire does here provides a microcosm of the work of the *philosophes* in setting reason against deep-seated cultural habit, against all the institutions that extinguish both the capacity for judgement, the responsibility for clear perception of the world, and a natural empathy.

## The tension between social façade and inner nature

One of the most enduring literary successes of the century, an immediate best-seller with continued broad appeal (and the basis of at least four films), was Pierre Choderlos de Laclos's epistolary novel *Les Liaisons dangereuses* (1782). One of the characteristics of the epistolary form makes it particularly hard to locate a message or intention in any simple way, since there is no overall narrative voice. The book has variously been seen as anti-aristocratic (this is how the book was perceived by many of Laclos's contemporaries), feminist, anti-feminist, moralistic, and immoral. As a collection of letters set mostly in chronological order, the work at first seems to offer neutrality in point of view, but the letters written by the two highly self-conscious dominant characters, the Vicomte de Valmont and the Marquise de Merteuil (dominant both in the number of letters they write – though there are twice as many from Valmont – and in their clever manipulation of the other letter writers), essentially take up the functions of the narrator in a conventional single-narrator novel. They not only tell what happens, but analyse motivations and predict outcomes. We can consider the novel as having, therefore, two non-omniscient narrators who are competing with each other not only to present a certain view of what happens but to make things happen. Both are cynical rationalists with a keen understanding of human nature (that is, patterns of behaviour) but with blindspots that lead them both to ruin. We can see echoes of La Rochefoucauld in this psychology; Merteuil explicitly states that she learned about life by reading the works of 'the most severe moralists', and La Rochefoucauld was especially acute in noting that people are blind to their own susceptibilities and motivations. Although Valmont and Merteuil consider themselves completely emancipated from religion and morality, they need to adjust appearances in order to function within the codes of their society, codes that are different for men and for women. For Valmont, as a male libertine, a public reputation as a successful seducer of women is a source of pride and has little negative impact on him. For Merteuil, it is quite different. She needs to seduce imperceptibly and always in circumstances that maintain for her a public reputation as a pious young widow. Even the men she seduces must not know that she has seduced them but must believe that they have seduced her. The unequal status accorded to men and women by society is thus an important theme and one that, along with the portrayal of a corrupt and idle aristocracy, is representative of the contemporary questioning of social convention and education.

By the end of the novel, Valmont's and Merteuil's rivalry (the smouldering remains of an earlier love affair between them) leads them to take vengeance on each other. Merteuil does this in the more subtle fashion by exploiting the gap between Valmont's gendered self-perception as publicly successful libertine seducer, on the one hand, and his real and passionate love for Madame de Tourvel, his most difficult conquest to date. Valmont, as Merteuil saw, is blind to his own nature. Confident in his rationalist stance, he believes that physical pleasure and virtuosity in seduction are his only motives. By exploiting the vanity that is indissociable from this form of male self-image, Merteuil provokes Valmont to destroy his only chance at emotional fulfilment. Valmont's subsequent revenge upon Merteuil is much cruder and easier and is also based on the gender disequilibrium created artificially by society. He simply leaves the packet of letters to be published, thus making her a pariah. The discrepancy between Valmont's deepest emotion and his socially determined vanity marks *Les Liaisons dangereuses* as valorizing nature over the social norms that alienate people from their deeper, hidden selves.

## Flora, fauna, and 'nature'

Laclos's novel is concerned with human nature in the form of what we would call psychology. What counts is the social world, and the changes of place from Paris to a country manor are only described as they inflect the interactions among groups of people – in this respect, Laclos's work is closer to novels of the preceding century. But many writers of the 18th century reflect an explosively growing interest in non-urban spaces and contextualize human behaviour and perception along a city/country divide. By mid-century, the work of the Swedish botanist Carl Linnaeus had reached France, and it became increasingly fashionable to *herboriser*, that is, to look for plant specimens. Buffon (Georges-Louis Leclerc, comte de Buffon) published the first volume of his *Histoire naturelle, générale et particulière* in 1749. Flora and fauna from a wide variety of climates became of interest to the general public, and alongside the new importance accorded to plants and animals were the people who lived among them. Country dwellers were no longer seen exclusively as persons deprived of the advantages of the city, for the life of the fields and the forests now seemed to offer protection from the artifice and corrupting influences of the city. This is a significant extension of the image that Jean de La Bruyère, in his *Caractères, ou les moeurs de ce siècle* (1688), drew of the pitiless and soul-less artificiality of Parisian and court life. La Bruyère portrayed the culture of his time as corrupting and created caustic images of the artificiality of the upper classes, but did not go so far as to suggest that things are really better outside the court and the city. Rousseau extended his critique of urban civilization, already set forth in the *Discourse on the Origins of Inequality*, in his *Letter to d'Alembert on Spectacles* (*J.J. Rousseau Citoyen de Genève, à Mr. d'Alembert sur les spectacles*, 1758), in which he denounced the corrupting Parisian theatre in favour of the honest festivities of the 'happy peasants' in the small cities of the provinces. Childhood took on a new importance with Rousseau – it continues to be a significant interest for the Romantics, starting with Chateaubriand. Rousseau devotes a great deal of attention to his own childhood in his autobiographical *Confessions* (finished in 1769, but published in 1782). And in *Émile ou De l'éducation* (1762), an exemplary narrative of a radically new form of upbringing, Rousseau, in the role of tutor, permits his young pupil only one book, Defoe's *Robinson Crusoe*, in the hope that Émile will model himself on the self-reliant Crusoe living in a state of 'nature'.

In 1788, the year before the meeting of the *États Généraux* at Versailles, which is customarily seen as the beginning of the Revolution, Rousseau's younger friend Bernardin de Saint-Pierre (1737–1814), an engineer, published one of the best-selling novels of the 18th century, *Paul et Virginie*. It is the quintessence of the nature versus culture theme of its time

5. A scene from Bernardin de Saint-Pierre's novel *Paul et Virginie* (1787), in a 1805 engraving after François Gérard

and created, in Virginie, a heroine whose abandonment of the simpler ways of her childhood upbringing in the wilderness leads directly to her death. The action of the novel takes place in Mauritius, then known as the Île de France, where as children, Paul and Virginie grow up as best friends and almost siblings. At adolescence, their feelings change to romantic love, but Virginie is sent away to live in France with a wealthy and elderly aunt. When the aunt tries to force Virginie into a marriage, she refuses and is sent back to the island. As the ship nears land, a hurricane strikes and grounds the boat. The last sailor on the vessel tries to convince the heroine to take off her encumbering dress and swim to the land, but she refuses and accepts her fate. The author is emphatic on this matter of clothing and the quite dysfunctional modesty that Virginie brought from her European education. Modern readers may be tempted to laugh at the pathetic description of her corpse: 'Her eyes were closed; but the pale violets of death intermingled on her cheeks with the roses of modesty. One of her hands was on her dress, and the other, clutched to her heart, was tightly closed...'. She grasps, of course, Paul's portrait.

Bernardin brought together, as did Rousseau, the concepts of human nature and of nature in the sense of flora and fauna, setting up the romantic idea that nature exists in a special way in certain places, that by leaving the city one comes closer to 'nature', and by leaving Europe altogether one might find nature unspoiled – or one might, at the very least, come to a new understanding of oneself and of society by having a different vantage point. Paul and Virginie develop as upright, generous, frank, and somewhat austere young people not only because they are spared the corrupting social influences of their contemporaries in Europe but also, more mysteriously, because they are close to the earth of their tropical island. The contention that the basic trope of the novel as a genre is metonymic rather than metaphoric (that is, that it conveys significance by associating things in terms of spatial proximity rather than similarity) is useful for an understanding of the use of description in *Paul et Virginie* (and as it will be subsequently for the novels of Sand, Flaubert, and Balzac). Not only do the descriptions of plants and landscapes give an idea of the heroine's and hero's temperaments, but the interaction with these places shapes these temperaments. In the spirit of Rousseau's *Émile*, Paul is fully capable of felling a tree without an axe, making a fire without a flint, and making a warm meal from a palm bud. Paul, in short, seems an avatar of Robinson Crusoe. His greatness depends on what he can do, not on his birth.

# Chapter 5

# Around the Revolution

> 'Because you are a great lord, you think you are a genius!…Nobility, wealth, rank, estates, all that makes you so proud! What did you do for so many riches? You simply took the trouble to be born, and nothing more: otherwise, a fairly ordinary man!'
>
> (*Parce que vous êtes un grand seigneur, vous vous croyez un grand génie!…Noblesse, fortune, un rang, des places, tout cela rend si fier! Qu'avez-vous fait pour tant de biens? Vous vous êtes donné la peine de naître, et rien de plus: du reste, homme assez ordinaire!*)

With these words in a soliloquy, Figaro, the valet to Count Almaviva, describes his master, in Pierre Caron de Beaumarchais's masterpiece *The Crazy Day, or The Marriage of Figaro* (*La Folle journée, ou Le Mariage de Figaro*), which was finally performed at the Comédie Française on 27 April 1784 after six years of censorship and intrigue. Less than five years later, in January 1789, the *États Généraux* were called into session for the first time since 1614 and, with hindsight, we perceive this as the beginning of the French Revolution.

Beaumarchais's comedy has become symbolic of the cultural ferment that led to the Revolution, though, like all historical events, there is a certain arbitrariness in choosing one single moment as the 'beginning'. The 18th century as a whole was full of signals

of a growing disaffection for an absolute monarchy, a growing
conviction that social institutions were based on an implicit
contract rather than on divine authority or on an unquestioned
nature of things. In the multi-talented Figaro, Beaumarchais
created an internationally recognized personage who incarnates
the wit, talent, and resentment of those who are not noble in title
but who form the enterprising and successful *tiers état* (the 'third
estate', as distinct from the aristocracy and the Church). Figaro has
at one point the audacity actually to call himself a *gentilhomme*,
explaining 'If Heaven had wanted, I would be the son of a prince' –
and his references elsewhere in the play to chance (*le hasard*) make
it clear that it is precisely a matter of pure chance that he and his
master the count occupy their actual positions.

Figaro is also the amusing barber of *The Barber of Seville* (*Le
Barbier de Séville*, 1775), in which work it is debatable whether he
is the central figure or in a supporting role, and the very fact that
he is the eponymous character and yet working for the benefit
of another points to tensions in both the literary and the more
broadly social context. In that earlier play, he helps the count
defeat the machinations of the ageing Dr Bartholo and marry
Bartholo's beautiful and wealthy young ward. The intricate and
extremely amusing goings-on in these two comedies are at least in
part responsible for the many works based on them, ranging from
Mozart's *Le nozze di Figaro* only two years after the play to one
of the early French films of Georges Méliès, *Le Barbier de Séville*
(1904), as is the resourcefulness of the protagonist. It is worth
noting that the titles of both comedies refer to Figaro.

Who is Figaro? The structure of *The Marriage of Figaro* places
this question somewhat unexpectedly in the middle of the play,
the third of the five acts, which consists of a judicial proceeding
to enforce a contract. Figaro had borrowed a large sum of money
from a much older woman and had promised to marry her if he
failed to repay the loan. In centring his play on this moment,
Beaumarchais emphasizes the themes of finance, contract, law,

birth, and class power – all themes that were central to the Revolution. Figaro's employer, the count, who is also trying to seduce Figaro's fiancée, is also the presiding judicial authority, and this arrangement calls into question the foundation of any just law. The only reason that Figaro is able to avoid this marriage is the chance discovery that he is the long-lost son of the woman from whom he borrowed the money. Figaro turns out to be of 'higher' birth than he had seemed, yet there is still a disparity between rank and talent. Figaro's question 'What did you do for so many riches?' remains a valid one, for it is clear that the powerful count is neither smarter nor more energetic than his valet and considerably less moral. Where Marivaux played with the idea that a person's intelligence, sensitivity, and talent might be at odds with his or her class (birth) origins, only to conclude in each case that, when the true identity of each is established, inherited privilege is justified, for Beaumarchais this is no longer the case.

When Figaro reclaims his birth identity in *The Marriage of Figaro*, Beaumarchais does more than reflect the political and social controversies of the day. He also points to the parallel agitation in literature itself. As Victor Hugo was to show a few decades later in the preface to *Cromwell*, the division of dramatic genres into comedy and tragedy no longer seemed to keep pace with perceptions of human society. The 18th century had burst out of this binary structure, inherited from 17th-century neo-Aristotelianism, and had produced many plays called *drames*. Beaumarchais himself had written a *drame*, *Eugénie*, that was performed at the Comédie Française in 1767, and on that occasion he also published his *Essay on the Serious Dramatic Genre* (*Essai sur le genre dramatique sérieux*). He again brought up this question in a 'Moderate Letter' (*Lettre modérée*) that he published as a preface to the printed version of *Le Barbier de Séville*. In this often sarcastic letter, he notes the classical distinction between comedy and tragedy and the traditional exclusion of anything in between. Aristotle had defined comedy as the representation of men lower than ourselves and tragedy as that of men superior to ourselves. Beaumarchais exclaims:

> To attempt to present people of a middle condition, overwhelmed and in wretched situations, shame on you! One should only show them ridiculed. Ridiculous citizens and unfortuante kings – those are the only real and possible theatrical works.
>
> (*Présenter des hommes d'une condition moyenne, accablés et dans le malheur, fi donc! On ne doit jamais les montrer que bafoués. Les citoyens ridicules et les rois malheureux, voilà tout le théâtre existant et possible.*)

The shift in dramatic genres corresponds, then, to a change in the type of person who can be the central figure, the hero, like Figaro.

## One extreme of the 'nature' debate

The century-long questioning of the basis of the social order and growing scepticism about the claims that the social order was founded on nature, itself based on divine providence, led to far more radical expressions. The Marquis de Sade (1740–1814) published *Justine ou les Malheurs de la Vertu* (1791) anonymously, the year after the Revolution brought about his release from a long imprisonment. *Justine* was an instant success. Although this novel, like most of his copious writings, is known for its depiction of the kind of sexual activity that gave us the adjective 'sadistic', Sade's writing concerns much more than 'unnatural' sexual practices. Anyone reading Sade primarily for titillation is likely to be disappointed: much of the narrative is interrupted by philosophical reflections on the permanence of evil and the pleasure that it gives the perpetrators. Although Sade took the side of the Revolution and was, despite his aristocratic origins, elected to the National Convention in 1790, he differed from the *philosophes* of the Enlightenment by not believing that society could bring about improvements in man's lot.

**6. Napoleon Bonaparte throwing a book of the Marquis de Sade into the fire, in a drawing attributed to P. Cousturier (1885)**

The liberation from revealed religion that permitted the Revolution to found a state on human reason was taken by Sade as the opportunity for complete freedom in the service of pleasure in a world in which the strong use and destroy the weak. One of the heroine's persecutors calmly explains the process by which primitive men invented a transcendent being to explain natural phenomena that frightened them. In its structure, *Justine* combines the loose, open-ended picaresque plot with the atmosphere of the gothic novel. Justine as heroine is a female Candide, but where Candide represents common sense at last freeing itself from a doctrine that is obviously ridiculous, in *Justine*, more daringly, the central tenets of religion and the traditional state are presented as absurd, while Justine tries vainly to resist on behalf of religion and virtue. In a dedicatory letter, Sade presents the triumph of vice as a literary innovation, saying that novels almost always show good rewarded and evil punished, but:

> to show an unfortunate woman wandering from one calamity to another, a plaything of wickedness, target of every debauchery, exposed to the most barbarous and monstrous appetites […] with the goal of drawing from all that one of the most sublime lessons of morality that mankind has every received – this is […] to reach the goal by a road little travelled until now.

Sade's atheistic libertinism was always out of step with the Revolution as a whole, with its emphasis on civic virtue and equality (both in short supply in Sade's novels) and became more so as time passed. Arrested by Napoleon under the Consulate, Sade died in the Charenton mental hospital just before the Bourbon Restoration.

## From 'heroes' to great men (and women)

'Men are born and remain free and equal in rights. Social distinctions can be based solely on what is useful to all' (*Les hommes naissent et demeurent libres et égaux en droits. Les distinctions sociales ne peuvent être fondées que sur l'utilité commune*), proclaims the first article of the Declaration of the Rights of Man and of the Citizen (*La Déclaration des droits de l'Homme et du citoyen*, 26 August 1789). This brief and eloquent official document, adopted by the National Constituent Assembly, demonstrates that the central issue of the struggle that lasted from 1789 until the Bourbon Restoration in 1814 was the status of each individual man (two years later Olympe de Gouges pointed out the omission of women's rights in her proposal for a *Déclaration des droits de la femme et de la citoyenne* – her text was rejected and she died on the guillotine in 1793).

Figaro had prefigured this demand for equality, and Justine suffered as eternal victim of an aristocratic libertinism. Looking forward and backwards from these representative literary figures, we can see (with help from Beaumarchais's *Moderate Letter*) that all works reveal ideas, usually implicit and taken for granted, about which people are worth writing about, about whose stories are important. The choice of central figure can fall on a hero, as in the case of Roland, who represents the highest aspirations of society as perceived by the author; on an eccentric, like Molière's misanthropic Alceste; or on a villain or anti-hero, consummate example of some deep vice, like the hypocrite Tartuffe in another comedy of Molière, *Le Tartuffe*. The Revolution broadened the spectrum of those whose stories were considered worthy of attention – following the line advocated by Beaumarchais, but not far enough for de Gouges – and it would continue to broaden in the following centuries. Nonetheless, it would be a vast simplification to say that French literature had simply become more 'egalitarian' and shifted from Roland to Figaro, from Gargantua to Candide. There had always been central characters who represented those of modest condition, from the street-smart self-taught lawyer Master Pierre Pathelin (in *La Farce de Maistre Pathelin*, c. 1464) to the police officers of Lyon in François de Rosset's *Histoires tragiques de nostre temps* (1614). However, these people were generally presented as either comical or shocking in a society within which literature reflected the unchanging assignment of people to life-long places within class (or 'condition'). While they might be protagonists, they were not 'heroes' if we mean by this term those who are held in highest esteem.

**7. Voltaire's remains are transferred to the Pantheon, 1791, engraving after Lagrenée**

The Revolution, following developments throughout the Enlightenment, changed that. On 4 April 1791, the Constituent Assembly ordered the transformation of the just-built church of the abbey of Sainte Geneviève into a 'Pantheon of Great Men' (*Panthéon des Grands Hommes*). This was a decisive shift, from the older concept of the 'hero' to the new idea of 'great man'. Henceforth, not only exceptional military valour but also outstanding merit in non-military service would be recognized as earning a place at the pinnacle of society. Heretofore, the highest aristocracy, from whom the monarch came, had been fundamentally a military caste (the *noblesse d'épée*), and one of the highest functions of the poet had been to sing the glory of the military hero. The physical monument known as the Pantheon (where today the writers Rousseau, Voltaire, Victor Hugo, Émile Zola, and André Malraux are buried) marks the culmination of this shift in the conception of greatness, and it has been shown that the Enlightenment idea of the 'great man' and of a national Pantheon preceded the architectural site that we now associate with that name.

## Literature and its epoch

Literature concerning the Revolution continued to be written long after the Bourbon kings returned. On this point, two observations should be made, one obvious and the other less so. It is obvious that in the quarter-century between the *États Généraux* of 1789 and the installation of Louis XVIII as king in 1814, less could be written about the events of those years than in the centuries that have followed. France thus has many novels, plays, and poems about the Revolution from the following period. A less obvious observation is that whenever we write about literature within an historical framework, it is difficult to resist the (false) idea that the French people of the past had available to them the same range of texts that we do. Of course, for the most part, they had more; they had the many books that were printed once and never reprinted or that were best-sellers at the time and then disappeared into the depths of the Bibliothèque Nationale de France. It has been said that there were well over a thousand plays produced during the Revolution – but (as Villon might have asked): where are the plays of yesterday?

On the other hand, in some instances we have works that contemporaries did not have. De Gouges's *Déclaration des droits de la femme et de la citoyenne* was printed in 1791, but how many people actually saw this proposal, which now figures in many university courses about Revolutionary France? In the case of Sade, his manuscript *Les Cent Vingt Journées de Sodome*, which he wrote in the Bastille and lost on his release, was not widely available in print until the 1930s. Should this work by Sade be considered part of the history of the literature of the 18th century, or of the 20th? Such questions, of course, are not limited to this particular period, nor even to unpublished or little-circulated works. Montaigne's *Essais* (first edition 1580; revised editions in 1588 and 1595) are routinely viewed as part of the literary culture of the 16th century. Yet the third book of the *Essais*, containing some of the most important chapters, could only have been read during the last 11 years of the 16th century, whereas Montaigne was a hugely important author during the century after his death. And Irène Némirovsky's novellas, written before the author died in Auschwitz, were published more than sixty years later as *Suite Française* (2004). They belong in one sense to the culture of the Second World War and the Holocaust, and in another sense to the literary culture of the early 21st century.

## Looking back at the Revolution

So the Revolution continued to inspire literary works in various and sometimes paradoxical ways, and to focus on characters who could not have been imagined prior to this great upheaval. Claire de Duras's short story *Ourika* (1823) appears in many ways as a very modern text that has affinities both with the anti-slavery and pro-woman writings of Olympe de Gouges and with today's feminism and interest in non-European cultures. On the other hand, the narrative *Ourika* emerges out of a highly conservative point of view that ends by condemning both the progressive aristocracy of the Enlightenment and the Revolution for creating excessive hope for emancipation. In her own terms, the central figure of the story, Ourika, is a kind of monster created by the Enlightenment and by an incomplete Revolution. Her first-person narrative (which is presented as committed to paper by an attending physician) relates her arrival in France as an orphan from Senegal who was bought as a slave at the age of two by a kind-hearted colonial governor and given to his aunt, who raised her as a beloved child. Ourika lives happily in luxury and is given a 'perfect education', learning English, Italian, painting, and reading the finest authors. She knows that she is *une négresse* but is far from considering this a defect. Everyone finds her charming, elegant, and beautiful. She is an outstanding dancer. In short, everything seems wonderful to Ourika until the day when she overhears a conversation in which her generous patroness tells a friend about Ourika, 'I would do anything to make her happy, and yet, when I think about her position, I see it as hopeless. Poor Ourika! I see her as alone, forever alone in life!'

8. Bust by Jean-Baptiste Carpeaux, entitled 'Why be born a slave?' (1868)

From that point onward, Ourika realizes that her race makes her unmarriageable in a society in which only marriage can confer station, respectability, and an honourable relationship with a man. In the words of one of the characters in the story, Ourika's upbringing has 'violated the natural order' (*brisé l'ordre de la nature*). She could only marry an inferior, venal man who 'for the sake of money, would consent perhaps to have negro children'. Ourika ends up in a convent, ashamed both of the African slaves who revolted in Haiti and at the executions and confiscations of the Revolution in European France. She fits in nowhere except in the convent, neither in the old French, white aristocratic order in which she was raised, nor in her native Senegal, nor in the supposedly egalitarian democratic society. Claire de Duras, who hosted a very influential Paris salon during the Restoration, shows in *Ourika* the conservative or reactionary face of French Romanticism. This short narrative incorporates some of Rousseau's and Bernardin de Saint-Pierre's ideas of the harmful effects of society and the natural order – Ourika is like a Senegalese Virginie, lost when transported to Europe. But Duras's idea of the 'natural order' is an anti-Revolutionary one, belonging to the world of the Restoration aristocracy which returned to France from exile.

Many of these exiled aristocrats wrote with decided nostalgia for the old order, often going far back into the past for their settings or continuing the 18th-century exploration of exotic locations, but with an anti-Enlightenment, Christian emphasis like that presented by François-René de Chateaubriand, author of the very influential *The Genius of Christianity* (*Le Génie du Christianisme*, 1802). In his novella *René*, published originally as part of this longer work, he portrays the troubled hero René, a lonely, tormented, self-centred aristocrat, haunted by his incestuous love of his sister (here, again, the insistence on the tragic consequences of violations of the natural order), who finds truth among the North American Indians. René's flight to Louisiana may have been suggested by the earlier and extremely popular *Manon Lescaut*, by Antoine François Prévost (1731), in which the courtesan Manon – a prototype for many a subsequent 'femme fatale' – and her lover seek to live peacefully in the French colony, but where Manon dies of exposure and exhaustion in the inhospitable wilderness. Chateaubriand, a somewhat paradoxical follower of Rousseau, used the New World as the vantage point from which to criticize modern mankind: alienated, self-important, and without the humility to submit to tradition. With Chateaubriand, the ideas of the 'modern' and of progress take on meanings quite different from the ones they had before the Revolution. The Enlightenment had largely accepted from the 17th century the promotion of classical antiquity as far superior to the intervening Middle Ages. Chateaubriand accepted the idea of progress, but attributed it to Christianity, and thus shifted emphasis from antiquity to the centuries of Christian dominance. He engaged in a public controversy with the important theorist and critic Germaine de Staël, author, among many other works, of *On Literature Considered in its Relations with Social Institutions* (*De la littérature considérée dans ses rapports avec les institutions sociales*, 1800), in which he set out his strong opposition to any positive concept of modernity not based on Christianity. His revalorization of the medieval over the classical worldview had many followers in the 19th century.

On the other side of the political and cultural divide that issued from the Revolution is Stendhal (pen-name of Marie-Henri Beyle, 1783–1842), who served in the Napoleonic armies, and who created a kind of anti-René in Julien Sorel, hero of *The Red and the Black* (*Le Rouge et le noir, Chronique de 1830*, 1830), an ambitious young man of very modest class inspired by Napoleon, yet living under the oppressive Bourbon monarchy. As an adolescent, his favourite books are Rousseau's *Confessions* and *Le Mémorial de Sainte-Hélène*, an account of Napoleon's conversations during his last years as a prisoner, after his defeat at Waterloo. Stendhal, considered the forerunner of the 'realist' novel, both creates a fascinatingly complex character and evokes the long-lasting social tensions and turbulence that followed the Revolution up until the July Revolution (like Stendhal's novel, 1830). Although Julien's two dominant traits are hypocrisy and ambition, he is surrounded by women and men who love and help him during his social ascent and then his spectacular crime and execution. The contrast between his heroic aspirations – however anti-heroic the means he adopts to achieve them – and the philistinism, complacency, and greed of the society around him, is typical of the Romantic conception of the hero found soon after in Alfred de Vigny's play *Chatterton* (1835) and many works of the subsequent decades.

# Chapter 6

# The hunchback, the housewife, and the *flâneur*

As Stendhal's novel showed, the France of the early decades of the 19th century was divided politically and culturally between, on the one hand, the desire for reconnection to traditional institutions (such as the Roman Catholic Church, monarchy, the countryside and village) that imparted the sense that everyone had a relatively fixed place in the social order and, on the other hand, the aspiration to ideals of human potential, freedom, and universal rights. This dichotomy often took the concrete form of the opposition between Paris and *la province* (anywhere else in France; significantly, in French, this is expressed as a singular noun and conveys as much the sense of a condition as of a place).

## Nostalgia and history

The aftershocks of the French Revolution and the reactions against it continued to the very end of the 19th century – the Dreyfus Affair and Zola's resounding editorial 'J'Accuse!' in 1898 exposed the persistence of aristocratic privilege in France – but another revolution, the Industrial Revolution, was at work shaping French society and the perception of time, place, human relations, and human creations. Fascination with the Ancien Régime and the Christian cultural heritage, exemplified by Chateaubriand, became a trend, taking on greater historical weight through the work of historians like Jules Michelet, literary historians like Sainte-Beuve, and architects like Viollet-le-Duc. The latter is responsible for rebuilding (in ways that are now often seen as more fanciful than historically accurate) the cathedral of Notre Dame de Paris, the Mont Saint-Michel, and the fortified city of Carcassonne. Following upon the writings of Chateaubriand and de Staël, Victor Hugo vigorously asserted a theory of social and aesthetic progress in the preface to his drama *Cromwell* (1827), framed historically within the concept of three ages of human society – the primitive, the ancient or antique, and the modern – which correspond to the sequence of development of literary genres: lyric, epic, and dramatic.

The 'modern' period for Hugo is quite extensive, for he equates it with the dominance of Christianity in Europe. Drama was born on the day Christianity said to man:

> 'You are double, you are composed of two beings, one perishable, the other immortal; one carnal, the other ethereal; one chained to its appetites, needs, and passions, the other born up on the wings of enthusiasm and reverie; one always bent towards earth, its mother, the other always springing towards heaven, its homeland'. This is the day that drama was born.

From this concept of doubleness, Hugo derives an insistence on the mixed character of all modern art, which should depict the sordid as well as the sublime, the trivial as well as the important. In rejecting the drama of the 17th and 18th centuries, Hugo (like Stendhal in *Racine et Shakespeare*, 1823–4), saw the English dramatist as superior to the French tragedian because Shakespeare included the melancholic, the earthy, and the grotesque alongside the sublime. Accusing the French Academy and its neo-Aristotelian poetics of stifling Corneille's creativity, Hugo particularly praised the author of *Le Cid* as 'an entirely modern genius, imbued with the Middle Ages and Spain, forced to lie to himself and to throw himself into Antiquity'.

9. Engraving by Luc-Olivier Merson (1881) inspired by Victor Hugo's novel *Notre Dame de Paris* (1831)

## Heroes of the grotesque

The link between the grotesque and the medieval appears in
Hugo's *Notre Dame de Paris* (1831, fourteen years before the
restoration of the crumbling monument was undertaken, in
part because of the impact of Hugo's work) – a novel best known
in English as *The Hunchback of Notre Dame*. Although Hugo
disapproved of the English title, because for him the cathedral
itself was the central character, the association of a deformed
body and a generous spirit in the fictive late 15th-century
bell-ringer Quasimodo provides one example of the doubleness
that the author so prized. The hunchback first appears in the
novel when a festive crowd decides to elect its own 'pope of
fools' on the basis of the ugliest grimace. The contestants in turn
poke their faces through a broken circular window in a chapel
wall – thus, in effect, uniting the grimacing face with the stone
to suggest a gothic grotesque or gargoyle. Finally, a head appears
that is universally acclaimed. It is perfect: 'But then surprise and
admiration reached their pinnacle. The grimace was his face.
Or rather, his whole body was a grimace' (*Mais c'est alors que la
surpise et l'admiration furent à leur comble. La grimace était son
visage. Ou plutôt toute sa personne était une grimace*). This is
Quasimodo, who is both metonymically and metaphorically tied
to the cathedral itself: he is constantly present in the church, and
he is also similar to the building in its gothic aesthetic.

But the best-known dramatic example of this grotesque doubleness
is *Lorenzaccio*, Alfred de Musset's drama published seven
years after Hugo's preface to *Cromwell*. Neither *Cromwell* nor
*Lorenzaccio* were ever performed during their authors' lifetimes,
both were too incendiary by the standards of censorship of the
time, and both were, in their published form, considered impossible
to stage – Musset's play seems to require from sixty to a hundred
actors and extras. Musset based *Lorenzaccio* in part on a text by
his lover George Sand (Amandine Aurore Lucile Dupin, Baroness
Dudevant), a *scène historique* entitled *Une conspiration en 1537*.

Musset's work concentrates on the main hero's moral character, which at first seems, both to the audience and to almost all of his contemporaries within the play, to be entirely vicious. Completely absorbed in the pleasures of drink and sex, Lorenzo serves as procurer for his master and cousin, Alexandre, Duke of Florence, for whom he quickly and skilfully acquires the sexual services of the women of the city, by threats, promises, and money. A coward, he never carries a sword and is called by the Duke himself a *femmelette* (a 'womanling') after Lorenzo faints when challenged to a duel. As the scenes unfold, Lorenzaccio (the contemptuous form of the name that the Florentines have given him) seems entirely to merit everyone's scorn as bully, spy, toady, and coward. But then it appears that Lorenzaccio's character has been deliberately assumed for the purpose of killing Alexandre – in this way, Lorenzo would simply be a highly successful actor, concealing a unified and noble self. What makes Lorenzaccio fascinating to Musset, however, is something much darker: Lorenzo, the originally pure, studious, idealistic scholar of ancient Rome, who modelled himself on Lucius Junius Brutus, the killer of Tarquin, is not merely feigning to be vicious but rather he has really become Lorenzaccio.

Hugo's concept of a double man, both hideous and sublime, is realized in Musset's hero, who has really become addicted to the brutally licentious life while still aspiring to a heroic gesture of political and personal purity. We are led to suppose that what we have seen of Lorenzaccio in the first scene is not simply a feint but a true expression of his own desires:

> What is more curious for the connoisseur than to debauch an infant? To see in a child of fifteen the future slut; to study, seed, insinuate the thread of vice under the guise of a fatherly friend...
>
> (*Quoi de plus curieux pour le connaisseur que la débauche à la mamelle? Voir dans une enfant de quinze ans la rouée à venir; étudier, ensemencer, infiltrer paternellement le filon mystérieux du vice dans le conseil d'un ami...*)

Disseminating corruption throughout the families of Florence as within himself, Lorenzaccio has become such a cynic, or such a realist, in regard to human nature that his intention to follow through on his solitary plot to kill Alexandre has no connection whatever with the anti-tyrannical agitation among certain groups of Florentine families. In representing the character of the Florentines – and through them, no doubt, his 19th-century contemporaries – Musset shows that those who are outwardly 'noble' and quick to defend their honour are ineffectual. Lorenzaccio, outwardly despicable, manages to achieve the death of Duke Alexandre, though this really changes nothing. At the end of the play, as at the beginning, the Florentines complain and conspire, and life goes on as always.

## The provincial life

The exasperated sense that heroic striving is vain, and that the coarse, materialistic, conservative common sense of the bourgeoisie will always triumph over those who seek something more out of life often was embodied in the contrast between fast-changing, fashionable Paris and the stodgy, rustic, and boring provincial life. Balzac's immense collection of novels, which, in the course of its evolution, he decided to call *The Human Comedy* (*La Comédie Humaine*) is divided into various series and subseries that reflect the importance of the Paris – *province* distinction, such as the 'Scenes of the life of the provinces' (*Scènes de la vie de province*), the 'Scenes of Parisian life', and 'Scenes of country life'. Yet the greatest hero to strive against the prison of the provincial life is Emma Bovary, the protagonist of Gustave Flaubert's novel *Madame Bovary*.

When it first appeared as a serial in 1856 in the *Revue de Paris*, the work had the highly significant original title, *Madame Bovary, moeurs de province*. For Emma, a woman more intelligent than any of those around her, though with only a convent education, the most powerful magic is contained in the words, 'They do it in Paris!' (*Cela se fait à Paris!*), five words that suffice to propel her into the arms of her second lover. Paris is for her the ultimate place of dreams, though the dimension of place is insufficient without the figure of an ideal role or persona. Flaubert's novel is full of representations of the effect of representation, fictions that propel actions. Emma delights in heroines who come to her from stories told by the nuns, novels, magazines, and even from plates! As a child in the convent, 'they had supper on painted plates that depicted the story of Mlle de La Vallière' (the young mistress of Louis XIV, who once fled from the court to a convent). In her remote Norman village, Emma receives magazines from Paris, and she reads the novels of George Sand and Balzac. At one point, her mother-in-law tries to keep her from reading novels – a hint that Emma is a latter-day Don Quixote, maddened by reading. Her life cycles through fits of intense energy and striving to make something of herself, followed by periods of lethargy and sickness. This alternation contrasts with provincial routine, so regular in its seasonal cycles that it seems to be unchanged since time immemorial. Though she stands out from her milieu – and thus permits Flaubert to create a multitude of picturesque characters with all the acuity of a Dickens – Emma is neither a person of great intelligence nor refinement. Her unhappiness illustrates something said in Hugo's *Notre Dame de Paris*, 'A one-eyed man is much more incomplete than a blind one. He knows what he is missing' (*Un borgne est bien plus incomplet qu'un aveugle. Il sait ce qui lui manque*).

The view of *la province* conveyed in Flaubert (as in the novels of Stendhal and Balzac) shows that the cult of nature and of village life, so dear to followers of Rousseau and Bernardin de Saint-Pierre, had by mid-century provoked a backlash. There is nothing uplifting and noble about herding cows in Flaubert's work, and vistas of fields with flowers do not bring Emma any consolation. In fact, through Emma's cliché-ridden imagination, Flaubert parodies the romantic notion of an idyllic escape to the countryside when Emma fantasizes eloping with Rodolphe to 'a village of fishermen, where brown nets were drying in the wind, along a cliff with little huts. That is where they would settle down to live: they would have a low house with a flat roof, in the shade of a palm tree, at the end of a gulf, on the seaside'. This is both particularly comic and also very sad, in that Emma, who lives in the country, has internalized the fantasies of the city dweller she aspires to be.

Since Emma is a reader of Flaubert's friend and fellow novelist George Sand, it is difficult to resist comparing the character of Emma to the heroine of Sand's earlier work *Consuelo* (1842), a vast historical novel, set in the 18th century, that is almost picaresque in its structure though not in its tone. *Consuelo* follows the life of Consuelo from her impoverished childhood in Venice to her eventual marriage to the half-mad Bohemian (Czech) aristocrat Albert of Rudolstadt. Point by point, the two novels are entirely opposite: Emma is trapped in a prosaic French village, while Consuelo's life is almost a travelogue of the Austro Hungarian empire; Emma yearns for the aristocratic life and for the sophistication of the city and the theatre, while Consuelo spends a good deal of time fleeing all of these things. The life around Emma seems intensely boring but she tries to infuse it with excitement, while Consuelo's life is fully Romantic in the atmosphere and adventures that take place in medieval castles with subterranean passageways and gloomy forests. But most of all, the temperament of each heroine is directly opposed. Consuelo is goodness itself, always patient, generous, resourceful, caring for others, indifferent to wealth and prestige, and with no need for exotic escape.

## Urban exiles

'Any where out of the world', was Charles Baudelaire's diagnosis of human aspirations, so well represented by Emma Bovary and so foreign to Consuelo. The expression, in English, was the title of one of the prose poems in the volume *Le Spleen de Paris* (1869). In 'Any where out of the world', he evokes the power of the eternal 'elsewhere': 'This life is a hospital where each patient is obsessed with the desire to change beds'. This interest in what is happening in the other parts of the world/hospital is a key to the fascinating paradox that Flaubert, like Balzac, Sand, Stendhal, and others, could entertain sophisticated readers with stories of the supposedly stifling provincials, who, in turn, are shown to spend their time longing for Paris (or longing for village life as if they were Parisians). What could Parisians like Baudelaire find to interest them in the life of an unhappy provincial housewife?

Baudelaire was one of the many admiring readers of Flaubert's novel. In his review essay on *Madame Bovary* – which appeared several months after the trial that acquitted Flaubert for outrage to public and religious morality – Baudelaire described the novel as the triumph of the power of writing, a power so great that it scarcely needed a subject. Baudelaire either knew or intuited a famous formulation that Flaubert used in a letter to his lover Louise Colet five years earlier, saying that his dream was someday to write 'a book about nothing... that would have almost no subject or at least where the subject would be almost invisible' (1852). Baudelaire found in *Madame Bovary* the triumph of this artistic challenge: to take the most banal subject, adultery, in the place where stupidity and intolerance reign, *la province*, and to create a heroine who faces this 'total absence of genius' in a masculine way. This heroine, Madame Bovary herself, 'is very sublime in her kind, in her small milieu and facing her small horizon'. Baudelaire, in praising both Flaubert's novel and its heroine, seems at times to identify with her, despite the radical difference in places.

The quintessential Parisian poet, Baudelaire is almost unimaginable elsewhere, but this is not to say that he sings the praises of Paris. Having absorbed Hugo's teaching about the grotesque and about human doubleness, Baudelaire was fascinated by the ugly and by the sublime, by all that was unpredictable and out of place. Perfectly Parisian, Baudelaire, as both poet and as subject of his poetry, cultivated his sense of being in the wrong place as much as Emma Bovary did hers. He wrote of Emma that in her convent school she made for herself a 'God of the future and of chance', and one of the great values of the capital for Baudelaire was its capacity to produce random encounters that generated lyrical fusions.

It is understandable that the metropolis in mid-century should offer freedom and opportunity on a quite different scale from any other city in France, for it was growing explosively. In 1801, Paris had had virtually the same population as at the end of the 17th century, roughly half a million inhabitants in an area of less than 14 square kilometres. By the end of the century, the population quintupled, and Paris had annexed nearby towns and villages so that the urban area was eight times larger. Such an environment favours the 'God of chance' Baudelaire attributed to Emma Bovary, and he seized for himself a poetic persona well adapted to this moment, that of the stroller (*le flâneur*), a role that he describes in an essay on the painter Constantin Guys, 'The Painter of Modern Life': 'For the perfect stroller, for the passionate observer, it is an immense pleasure to dwell in the multitude, in the undulating, in movement, in the fleeting, and the infinite'. The sonnet 'To a Woman Passing By' (*À une passante*, in *Les Fleurs du mal* [*Flowers of Evil*]) illustrates the intensity and the chance nature of the encounters that the poet-stroller prizes in the immense, fast-moving, modern city. The two quatrains, with no addressee, describe a crowded street scene and then the vision of a striking woman. The tercets start by evoking the woman's glance, and then the poet addresses the woman directly. The lightning-like strike of the glance turns the poet's thoughts forward from this encounter to the improbability of future encounters, and shifts the sonnet into a thematic well known to Emma Bovary and her readers: the longed-for elsewhere and another time, when love is fulfilled. The single italicized word, *jamais* (never) – Baudelaire almost never used italics – stresses the other-worldly character of this time, which may not come in this life. The woman, who is in mourning, may indeed be Death, but she may also be simply a woman in the crowd whose ephemeral image nourishes the poet's imagination and to whom the poet attributes an equal role in this mental exchange. The very title of the poem suggests extremes, the fullness of life in a city in which people move rapidly and pass one another (as they do not in a village) and also the eventual absence of movement of someone who has passed beyond life – life and death themselves telescoped into the antithesis of a lighting flash followed by darkness.

A variant of Hugo's double man, the stroller is exquisitely attuned to time, and especially to the vanished past and to the dissonance

## À une passante

La rue assourdissante autour de moi hurlait,
Longue, mince, en grand deuil, douleur majestueuse,
Une femme passa, d'une main fastueuse
Soulevant, balançant le feston et l'ourlet;

Agile et noble, avec sa jambe de statue,
Moi, je buvais, crispé comme un extravagant,
Dans son oeil, ciel livide où germe l'ouragan,
La douceur qui fascine et le plaisir qui tue.

Un éclair... puis la nuit! – Fugitive beauté
Dont le regard m'a fait soudainement renaître,
Ne te verrai-je plus que dans l'éternité?

Ailleurs, bien loin d'ici! trop tard! *jamais* peut-être!
Car j'ignore où tu fuis, tu ne sais où je vais,
O toi que j'eusse aimée, ô toi qui le savais!

### To a Woman Passing By

The deafening road around me roared.
Tall, slim, in deep mourning, making majestic grief,

A woman passed, lifting and swinging
With a pompous gesture the ornamental hem of her garment,

Swift and noble, with statuesque limb.
As for me, I drank, twitching like an old roué,
From her eye, livid sky where the hurricane is born,
The softness that fascinates and the pleasure that kills,

A gleam, then night! O fleeting beauty,
Your glance has given me sudden rebirth,
Shall I see you again only in eternity?

Somewhere else, very far from here! Too late! Perhaps *never*!
For I do not know where you flee, nor you where I am going,
O you whom I would have loved, O you who knew it!

Translated by Geoffrey Wagner, *Selected Poems of
Charles Baudelaire* (New York: Grove Press, 1974)

of near misses. He lives vividly both in the Parisian present
and in the past and the elsewhere. In 'The Swan' (*Le Cygne*,
dedicated to Victor Hugo, 1860), Baudelaire builds his poem
around another chance encounter in a Paris undergoing the
colossal transformations that Haussmann carried out between
1853 and 1870 and that created the city of wide boulevards and
standardized building heights that we know today. In the process,
most of medieval Paris disappeared, thus endowing the vestiges
of the Middle Ages with a new, nostalgic, value.

In 'The Swan', Baudelaire creates a deft mosaic of different
moments, especially three: the present, in which he is crossing the
newly constructed Place du Carrousel between the Tuileries and
the Louvre; a past moment when there had been a menagerie in
that place; and the imagined moment in Greek antiquity when
the Trojan prince Hector's widow Andromache, become the
slave of Pyrrhus, bends over the cenotaph of her heroic husband.

10. Maxime Lalanne (1827–86), 'Demolition work for the construction of the Boulevard Saint-Germain', a scene from Haussmann's renovations of Paris

Baudelaire assembles these moments along the thematic axis of absence: in crossing the Carrousel, he sees that the menagerie is no longer there. In that menagerie, a swan had escaped from its cage, and vainly sought water from the dry pavement. The poet imagines the swan remembering the lost lake of its youth and then imagines Andromache remembering Hector. The last three quatrains of the poem evoke a myriad of others who have lost something, and specifically those who have lost a place, like the 'emaciated and tubercular Negress...seeking...the missing palm trees of proud Africa'. The stroller is thus the guise in which the city poet can multiply his experience of narrative characters, for he identifies himself with each in turn: Andromache, the swan, the African woman, and perhaps even with the dying hero of the *Song of Roland*: 'An old memory blows a horn with full force'.

The endless change that seemed to Baudelaire to be the only constant of Paris accelerated a decade after *Le Cygne*. The Franco-Prussian War of 1870–1 ended the Second Empire and brought the insurrection known as the Paris Commune and its bloody suppression. Paris almost tripled its surface area in the second half of the century, and the continued development of the rail network centred on the capital brought more workers.

11. Claude Monet, *La Gare Saint-Lazare* (1877)

One side of this change is reflected in the naturalist novels of Émile Zola (1840–1902) with their attention to the gritty underside of this prosperous period, the heyday of the French colonial empire. These include *L'Assommoir* (1877) and *La Bête humaine* (1890), both about the ravages of alcoholism in working-class families. But in reaction to naturalism in the novel and theatre came Symbolism, which found in Baudelaire its harbinger and in Stéphane Mallarmé its greatest exponent. Much of his poetry, in appearance frivolous and occasional (for instance, a series on women's fans, on a coiffure, etc.), concerns death and memorialization, particularly monuments to poets. With Ronsard and Hugo, Mallarmé is probably the poet who most vigorously championed the power of language itself to challenge death. Mallarmé's protagonists are therefore most often poets, celebrated in a series of sonnet 'tombs' such as *Le Tombeau d'Edgar Poe* (1876), but in time Mallarmé reached the highest point of abstraction with a protagonist named, simply, Igitur (Latin, 'therefore') in a posthumous prose text dating from around 1870, *Igitur, ou la folie d'Elbehnon*. The hero finishes in the tomb after challenging Nothingness with a roll of the dice: 'The character, who, believing in the existence of the Absolute alone, imagines himself everywhere in a dream [...] finds action unnecessary' (*Le personnage qui, croyant à l'existence du seul Absolu, s'imagine être partout dans un rêve [...] trouve l'acte inutile*). This text may be the earliest form of the great hermetic poem that Mallarmé published almost thirty years later, in which we seem to encounter once again Igitur's roll of the dice: *A Roll of Dice Will Never Abolish Chance* (*Un coup de dés jamais n'abolira le hasard*, 1897). In its graphic disposition, apparently spattered across the page in different fonts and type sizes, this is one of the most inventive texts in all of French literature, and it was crucially important for the following century.

LE NOMBRE

EXISTÂT-IL
autrement qu'hallucination éparse d'agonie

COMMENÇÂT-IL ET CESSÂT-IL
sourdant que nié et clos quand apparu
enfin
par quelque profusion répandue en rareté

SE CHIFFRÂT-IL

évidence de la somme pour peu qu'une

ILLUMINÂT-IL

# LE HASARD

*Choit*
*la plume*
*rythmique suspens du sinistre*
*s'ensevelir*
*aux écumes originelles*
*naguères d'où sursauta son délire jusqu'à une cime*
*flétrie*
*par la neutralité identique du gouffre*

12. A page of Stéphane Mallarmé's poem, *Un coup de dés jamais n'abolira le hasard* (1897)

# Chapter 7

# From Marcel to Rrose Selavy

## The world of Proust's novel

The heady metaphysical aspirations of Mallarmé's spare lyric, which seem at times ready to leave language and the printed page behind, appear at first to have little in common with the *roman-fleuve*, the immense, onward-streaming novel that marks the emphatic beginning of the 20th century, *In Search of Lost Time* (*À la recherche du temps perdu*, 1913–27) by Marcel Proust (1871–1922). Yet these two authors of the belle époque (a name given after the First World War to the preceding period of peace from the end of the Franco-Prussion War in 1870 until 1914) have in common an intellectual adventurousness nourished by the philosophical movements of the time. It is tempting to consider Proust's novel as a *Bildungsroman* (or as a variant thereof, the *Kunstlerroman* – the education of the artist), but one in which the usual linearity of that form has yielded to an extremely complex interplay of moments of experience and later moments of interpretation. This complexity is augmented by length, competing editions based on different opinions concerning the proper use of posthumous material, and different English translations with different titles. *À la recherche du temps perdu*, which in the current French Pléaide edition runs (with extensive notes) to more than 7,000 pages, is comprised of seven titled sub-novels. The first of these (published at the author's expense in

1913), *Swann's Way* (*Du côté de chez Swann*), contains the further
subsections *Combray, Swann in Love* (*Un amour de Swann*),
and *Noms de pays: le nom*. The last of the seven sub-novels, *Le
temps retrouvé*, was published in 1927, five years after Proust's
death. The novel – *À la recherche du temps perdu* – in terms of
the chronological range covered stretches from these childhood
memories of Combray, at the earliest, to the post-war Paris scenes
of the last novel in the series, *The Past Recaptured* (*Le temps
retrouvé*, literally 'time refound').

*Combray*, the very first section, opens with the narrator's
account of going to sleep and waking – the startling first
sentence is 'For a long time, I went to bed early' (*Longtemps,
je me suis couché de bonne heure*). The reader has no way of
knowing who is making this statement – and, in fact, the given
name of the protagonist is mentioned only rarely throughout
the seven narratives that make up the work as a whole – but
it becomes clear very quickly that there is something very
capacious and mysterious about this 'I'. Having fallen asleep
while reading, he writes, he would sometimes wake a half-
hour later still thinking about the book he was reading. But
these thoughts often took a peculiar form: 'it seemed to me
that I was the thing the book was about: a church, a quartet,
the rivalry between François I and Charles V' (*il me semblait
que j'étais moi-même ce dont parlait l'ouvrage: une église, un
quatuor, la rivalité de François Ier et de Charles-Quint*). For
several pages, the narrator pursues this investigation into the
contents of the mind at its awakening, with comments on the
identification of the thinking subject with a series of radically
heterogeneous objects. The fact that the mind does not at first
see them as objects but simply as part of itself is, for the reader,
most striking. The narrator continues by tracing the phases of
disengagement as the thinker rejoins the world of wakefulness
and can no longer understand the dream thoughts that at first
seemed so innocently obvious.

These opening pages of the novel, with the radical questioning of the boundaries of the self, have roots with a deep hold on the tradition of French literature. Montaigne, in a famous passage of the *Essais*, recounted his experience of returning to consciousness after a fall in the chapter 'On Practice' (*De l'exercitation*), as did Rousseau in one of his *Reveries of the Solitary Walker* (*Rêveries du promeneur solitaire*). Descartes, in his *Discourse on Method* (*Discours de la méthode*, 1637) had also tried stripping the consciousness of the self back to the simple awareness of being that precedes any actual knowledge of the qualities of that thinking self. In Proust's day, this Cartesian questioning had been given a new currency by the teachings of Franz Brentano and his two brilliant students, Edmund Husserl and Sigmund Freud. And Proust was certainly aware of the work of Henri Bergson, whose writings on the awareness of time have been frequently compared with Proust's work. Though Proust probably reached his interest in the phenomenology of the waking self independently, it is hard to deny that he brought a new vigour and concreteness to the exploration of consciousness, sensation, and memory.

He also gave a new prominence to childhood. The opening meditation on going to bed and waking leads into an account of the bedtime ritual during family summer vacations in Combray. To distract the child from the anguished separation from his mother that bedtime entailed, his family would let him project a magic lantern display onto the walls of his room, where Golo, the hero of the legendary tale represented by the images, exhibits the ability to morph himself according to the object on which he is projected – door knob, curtains, walls: 'Golo's body itself... dealt with any material obstacle, with any bothersome object that it encountered, by taking it as its skeleton, incorporating it, even the doorknob' (*Le corps de Golo lui-même... s'arrangeait de tout obstacle matériel, de tout objet gênant qu'il rencontrait en le prenant comme ossature et en se le rendant intérieur, fût-ce le bouton de la porte...*). Thus Marcel's ability, as the adult narrator,

French Literature

to imagine his waking self as a church or as the rivalry between the king and the emperor is prefigured in the child's experience of the hero's image in the lantern display as it transcends times and places in order to be himself. While Freud was, by another approach, teaching the long-term impact of childhood experience, Proust knit together childhood and adulthood in this persistence of narrative patterns and in the ability of people to identify – and to identify with – the protagonist's role.

This ability appears in the narrator's account of Swann, an adult friend of young Marcel's family, a Parisian who, like Marcel's parents, has a country house in Combray. As a child, Marcel dreads Swann's arrival for dinner parties because this means that his bedtime ritual will be perturbed, his mother will be occupied with her duties as hostess. In short, Swann appears as the cause of the terrible suffering due to the absence of the loved one. As an adult, however, Marcel sees that Swann would have known better than anyone what that suffering was like, for he suffered also from his love for Odette de Crécy. This treatment of Swann is simply an example of Marcel's characteristic plasticity as narrator – but also as protagonist – to focus on a wide range of people, of whom he discovers different aspects as he grows older. The fascination that appears in the early realization that 'Golo' could be himself but also a doorknob is the force that gives value to the subsequent realizations that people, attitudes, actions, and places that at first seemed entirely distinct and incompatible are, in fact, united. For instance, the paths in Combray that lead towards Swann's house (that is, that go *du côté de chez Swann*) seem at first to be entirely opposite those that go towards the château de Guermantes, and Swann and the aristocratic Guermantes family seem quite separate, but they are later shown to be connected. However, as even his perception of the spatial organization shows, the narrator's greatest talent is in creating unforgettable people. So that any reader of *À la recherche du temps perdu* is likely to carry around a mental repertory with characters such as Françoise the cook, Tante Léonie, Baron Charlus, Saint-Loup, Albertine, Elstir the painter, and so forth. These all flow out of the *moi* of the narrator himself, who becomes a super-character and the repository of the entire world that he recounts. Among the most moving pages of the novel are in the concluding section, *Le temps retrouvé*, where he realizes that the past is not gone because it still lives in him.

## The heritage of Mallarmé

Proust's contemporary Paul Valéry (1871–1945) was of a radically different aesthetic temperament. In contrast to the former's lengthy novel with its notoriously long and involved sentences (some spreading over several pages), Valéry's texts, both in prose and verse, are all very spare. Among the more unusual protagonists of French literature is his Monsieur Teste, the hero of a series of texts – one could call them prose poems or essays – in which Valéry explores his intellect in the form of an alter-ego, whose name evokes both 'head' (*tête*, or *teste* in older French) and 'text' (*texte*). Likewise in his verse poems, Valéry represents a self, a *moi*, that borders on the metaphysical. The closest heir of Mallarmé, and the last great Symbolist poet, Valéry's single greatest poetic achievement is *The Graveyard by the Sea* (*Le Cimetière marin*, 1920). Like much contemporary painting (one might think of Kandinsky), this verse poem in 24 stanzas evokes an event or scene that is then distilled to its essence, so much so that the physical incident is scarcely glimpsed. In *The Graveyard by the Sea*, the poet seems to describe an epiphany that he has during hours of thought while looking out at the Mediterranean from a cemetery. The question that he ponders is the relation between body, mind, and time (themes that run throughout the *Teste* texts also), with a concluding acceptance of the body and the demands and pleasures of physical life. More immediately accessible is the brief poem 'The Footsteps' (*Les Pas*), published a year after *The Graveyard*.

### Les Pas

Tes pas, enfants de mon silence,
Saintement, lentement placés,
Vers le lit de ma vigilance
Procèdent muets et glacés.

Personne pure, ombre divine,
Qu'ils sont doux, tes pas retenus!
Dieux!…tous les dons que je divine
Viennent à moi sur ces pieds nus!

Si, de tes lèvres avancées,
Tu prépares pour l'apaiser,
À l'habitant de mes pensées
La nourriture d'un baiser,

Ne hâte pas cet acte tendre,
Douceur d'être et de n'être pas,
Car j'ai vécu de vous attendre,
Et mon coeur n'était que vos pas.

### The Footsteps

Your footsteps, children of my silence,
With gradual and saintly pace
Towards the bed of my watchfulness,
Muted and frozen, approach.

Pure one, divine shadow,
How gentle are your cautious steps!
Gods!…all the gifts that I can guess
Come to me on those naked feet!

If, with your lips advancing,
You are preparing to appease
The inhabitant of my thoughts
With the sustenance of a kiss,

Do not hasten the tender act,
Bliss of being and not being,
For I have lived on waiting for you,
And my heart was only your footsteps.

Translated by David Paul

'The Footsteps' gives a very good idea of the way Valéry plays on the threshold of the physical and the metaphysical in much of his poetry. The poem is addressed to a 'pure person'. Is this a woman or a spirit? Is the 'divine shadow' literally divine, or is this hyperbole? Are the footsteps meant to be actual footsteps, or are they the metric feet of the poem itself? Or are the *pas* the poet's heartbeats (he says that his heart is nothing other than these *pas*), which he can hear because all is silent around him? And when those *pas* cease, it seems that the poet, as well as the poem, will come to an end. These are the kinds of questions that Valéry's poems provoke and that create opportunities for patient meditation, which for Valéry was a distinct superiority of poetry over the 19th-century novel.

## Surrealism

Valéry's acquaintance André Breton also reacted against the novel as genre, and *Nadja* (1928; revised edition 1962) is one alternative that he proposed. Breton's work is significant because of his role as leader of the Surrealists, a movement that reflected the continent-wide hunger for something new to replace both 19th-century literature and art and also the social order that had led to the butchery of the First World War. French Surrealism appears in the context of such other movements as Italian Futurism (already launched before the war but with its major impact in the decades thereafter), British Vorticism, Soviet Constructivism, the German Bauhaus, and Swiss and French Dadaism. André Breton was the author of the two *Surrealist Manifestos* (in 1924 and in 1929), thus becoming the public leader of the most significant of these movements (by 'movement' here is meant a group of writers who designate themselves as such and advocate a set of aesthetic and social doctrines). Breton advocated giving priority to the imaginative life and considered the 'real' life as most people know it to be only a pale reflection of the much more real (*surréel*, 'above real') life that was to be achieved upon the overthrow of narrowly rationalist forms of thought and the rejection of the limited options of adult life. In such a limited, ordinary person, dominated by practical concerns:

> All his gestures will be paltry, all his ideas narrow. He will only consider, in what happens to him and can happen to him, only the links to a mass of similar events, events in which he did not participate, *missed* events.
>
> (*Tous ses gestes manqueront d'ampleur; toutes ses idées, d'envergure. Il ne se représentera, de ce qui lui arrive et peut lui arriver, que ce qui relie cet événment à une foule d'événements semblables, événements auxquels il n'a pas pris part, événements* manqués.)

The life of the imagination, which most of us have lost, is cruelly rich in possibilities. In an apostrophe, Breton exclaims, 'Dear imagination, what I love above all about you is that you do not forgive' (*Chère imagination, ce que j'aime surtout en toi, c'est que tu ne pardonnes pas*). The world of imagination, for Breton, is not in the elaborate and carefully wrought creations of the novelists and poets of the tradition but, instead, in the everyday world that surrounds us without our noticing it. Breton was an early and enthusiastic reader of Sigmund Freud (as one can see from the term 'missed events' – coined on the model of the French term for what we call the lapsus or 'Freudian slip', an *acte manqué*), an admirer of Alfred Jarry's *Ubu Roi* (1896) and of Lautréamont's *Chants de Maldoror* (printed in 1868 but little known until the 1920s), and he promoted the concept of 'automatic writing' (*écriture automatique*), first practised in the collection of poetic

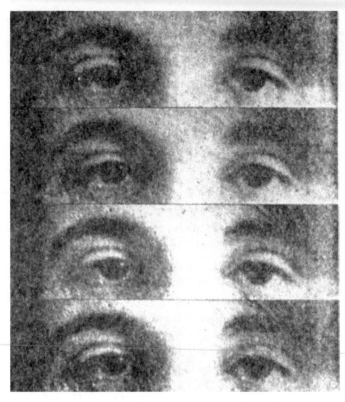

13. 'Les yeux de fougère', photographic montage illustration for André Breton's *Nadja* (1928)

prose *Magnetic Fields* (*Les Champs magnétiques*, 1919, with Philippe Soupault), as a way of breaking out of traditional forms and rationalist thinking.

Given Breton's preference for writing that eschewed any form of premeditation, moral censorship, and respect of traditional genres, it is not surprising that he assigned great weight to the creative role of chance in life. This is illustrated in his text *Nadja*, which is sometimes called a 'novel', though Breton fulminated against the tradition of the novel and stated that it was simply the record of real events, centred on his chance encounter with a young woman who called herself Nadja (though she made it clear that this was not her real name). He perceived in Nadja various parapsychological powers, and in answer to his question 'Who are you?', she answers, 'I am the wandering soul' (*Je suis l'âme errante*). He meets her several times, often by chance, and as they wander through Paris, each place becomes heavy with half-explained significance, suggesting that Nadja, at least, has had a previous existence in some of these locations. They dine in the Place Dauphine and later find themselves, by chance, in a café named 'Le Dauphin'; Breton explains that he had often been identified with the sea-mammal of the same name, the dolphin. Breton's respect for the reality of these Parisian places can be seen in the 48 photographs that are integrated into the text, some of them reproducing drawings made by Nadja, but most representing locations such as the Hôtel des Grands Hommes in the Place du Panthéon, Place Dauphine, the *Humanité* bookstore, the Saint-Ouen flea market, and so forth. These photographs ostensibly serve to avoid the lengthy descriptions that are so much a part of 19th-century realist and naturalist novels, but, since Breton does also describe things and people in words, they seem to have another purpose, or at least the effect, of preserving objects that have an almost talismanic importance for the author.

Breton's slim volume – *Nadja* is closer in size to a pamphlet than to most novels – does have at least one thing in common with Proust's sprawling work. Both authors consider the everyday world to be a source of great fascination and continue the progress of an ever greater inclusiveness in what can be deemed worthy of description and narration. For Proust, asparagus, diesel exhaust, and homosexual brothels figure alongside gothic churches and chamber music, while Breton found flea markets, film serials, and advertisements important to include in his text. Even more important is the role these authors give to involuntary mental processes in aesthetic creation. In a celebrated passage of *À la recherche du temps perdu*, Proust's narrator Marcel attributes the rediscovery of the events of childhood to the unpremeditated flash of memory that occurs upon tasting a madeleine dipped in a cup of linden tea. This aesthetic of *mémoire involontaire* is comparable to Breton's intention, as he stated it in *Nadja*, to tell of his life:

> to the extent that it is subject to chance events, from the smallest to the greatest, where reacting against my ordinary idea of existence, life leads me into an almost-forbidden world, the world of sudden connections, petrifying coincidences, reflexes heading off any other mental activity...

## An innovative novel from the right

Not all great shifts in writing come out of manifestos and self-proclaimed movements. In terms of prose style, *Journey to the End of Night* (*Voyage au bout de la nuit*) by Louis-Ferdinand Céline (1894–1961, born Louis-Ferdinand Destouches) had great impact on the diction of novels in the decades following its publication in 1932. And in addition to its influence on style, it contributed to the deflation of the protagonist's claim to the status of 'hero' in the noble sense. In this first-person novel, which begins with the First World War, the tough-talking, acerbic, working-class young narrator, Ferdinand Bardamu (the surname matches the author's and will be the name of the protagonist in Céline's subsequent novel, *Death on the Installment Plan* (*La mort à crédit*, 1936)), quickly decides that the war is a pointless butchery and gets himself hospitalized for mental illness, essentially for fear. He is, in short, anything but heroic, since the examples of heroism he sees around him seem to spring from lack of imagination or simple stupidity. Finding himself in a military hospital where the director's therapeutic idea is to infuse his patients with patriotic sentiments, Bardamu adapts by feigning compliance and even tells stories that become the basis for the recital of his 'heroic' adventures at the

Comédie Française. Wandering from Flanders to Paris, and then to West Africa, and from there to the United States, and finally back to Paris, where he becomes a medical doctor, Bardamu is a kind of Candide without the burden of an imposed philosophy. In fact, he is immune to almost every grand scheme of values, a precursor to the literature of the 'absurd' that became a recognized trend twenty years later. He serves, like Voltaire's character, as a critical lens through which to denounce American capitalism and the French military and colonial classes, and literature itself as vehicle of heroism. There is something Pangloss-like about the psychiatrist crowing about the recognition his method has received – 'I say that it is admirable that in this hospital that I direct has been formed under our very eyes, unforgettably, one of these sublime creative collaborations between the Poet and one of our heroes' (*Je déclare admirable que dans cet hôpital que je dirige, il vienne se former sous nos yeux, inoubliablement, une de ces sublimes collaborations créatrices entre le Poète et l'un de nos héros!*) – but Bardamu, who, after all, is narrator of this story, is the very first to see through all this hokum. Céline's narrator's corrosive, wordplay-filled descriptions achieve their goal of demystification by drowning the grandiose in the trivial or gross. Manhattan banks appear to him as hushed churches in which the tellers' windows are like the grills of confessionals, and only a few paragraphs later Bardamu describes the efforts of 'rectal workers' (*travailleurs rectaux*) in a public toilet.

Céline's use of slang and of the rhythms of popular, working-class speech are matched with a kind of narrow-focus narrative sequencing that keeps Bardamu's attention fixed on small details, while provoking the reader to extract from all of this the ideological significance of this additive critique. In various ways, Céline's innovations had a strong impact both on his younger contemporaries, like Albert Camus (in *L'Étranger*), and on much later writers such as Marie Darrieussecq (in *Truismes*). The huge and lasting fame of *Journey to the End of Night* has not been diminished by Céline's anti-Semitism and subsequent ties to the pro-Nazi Vichy regime (he was, after the war, declared a 'national disgrace'). However, the populist hero Bardamu, who had declared that 'the war was everything we didn't understand' (*la guerre en somme c'était tout ce qu'on ne comprenait pas*), has remained much more alive for the reading public than the contemporary anti-war heroes of another First World War novel, Roger Martin du Gard's *L'Été 1914* (1936, part of the longer work *Les Thibault*, 1922–40), for which Martin du Gard won the Nobel Prize for Literature in 1937. Perhaps, besides the inventiveness and the biting dark humour of Céline's work, this enduring success among anti-war novels is due to Bardamu's dead-pan cynicism, which seems closer to common perceptions of reality than the idealism of Martin du Gard's idealistic pacifist Jacques Thibault.

## The Second World War and the camps

Although Céline continued to write after the Second World War, his fame depends essentially on *Voyage au bout de la nuit* and *La mort à crédit*, because during and after the war, Albert Camus and Jean-Paul Sartre began to occupy some of the same terrain of populist critique and to provide coherent philosophical contextualization for the scepticism and anger that rolled so unpredictably through Céline's work. The war itself, and the German camps, ended the lives of many authors and changed the lives of others. It helped to form lasting institutions like the publishing house Minuit ('Midnight'), which had published works clandestinely during the war before becoming a major post-war press. The war ended much that was playful and experimental in the *entre-deux-guerres* period, and Robert Desnos (1900–45, died of typhus in Theresienstadt) is probably the best example. Editor of the review *La Révolution Surréaliste* from 1924 to 1929, Desnos published abundantly, drawing on the popular culture of Paris and on pulp crime serials such as *Fantômas*.

An illustration of the way ideas circulated as jokes within Surrealist circles is the character Rrose Selavy, who appears,

*loringly*
*Rrose Sélavy*
*alias Marcel Duchamp*

**14. Marcel Duchamp as Rrose Selavy, c. 1920–1, in a photograph by Man Ray**

among other places, in Desnos's 1939 book *Rrose Sélavy: oculisme de précision, poils et coups de pieds en tous genres* (*Precision Oculism, Complete Line of Whiskers and Kicks*). It was the multimedia artist Marcel Duchamp who created 'Rrose Selavy' in 1920 as an alter-ego. Duchamp was photographed in drag as 'Rrose' by Man Ray, and then Desnos made 'her' a character threaded through some of his poems, even as late as June 1944, just a year before his death. In 'Springtime' (*Printemps*, June 1944), we see the formerly playful figure now remembered as belonging to the imagination of a former time, or of a time that may come again later, after the poet's death in the theatre of war.

### Printemps

Tu, Rrose Sélavy, hors de ces bornes erres
Dans un printemps en proie aux sueurs de l'amour
Aux parfums de la rose éclose aux murs des tours,
à la fermentation des eaux et de la terre.

Sanglant, la rose au flanc, le danseur, corps de pierre
Paraît sur le théâtre au milieu des labours.
Un peuple de muets d'aveugles et de sourds
applaudira sa danse et sa mort printanière.

C'est dit. Mais la parole inscrite dans la suie
S'efface au gré des vents sous les doigts de la pluie
Pourtant nous l'entendons et lui obéissons.

Au lavoir où l'eau coule un nuage simule
A la fois le savon, la tempête et recule
l'instant où le soleil fleurira les buissons.

### Springtime

You, Rrose Sélavy, wander out of these bounds,
In a springtime haunted by the sweats of love,
By the scent of a rose that grows in the walls of the towers,
by the ferment of the waters and the earth.

Bleeding, the rose in his side, the rock-bodied dancer
Appears in the theatre, hard-ploughed.

A people of mutes, blind and deaf,
will applaud his dance and his vernal death.

Agreed. But the word traced in the soot
Fades at the whimsy of winds and rain-fingers
Yet we hear it and obey.

In the wash-house, where waters flow, double-dealing cloud
Feigns soap and timely tempest, adjourns
the instant of sun-blossomed bushes.

# Chapter 8

# The self-centred consciousness

Published in the midst of the Second World War, *The Stranger* (*L'Etranger*, 1942) belongs to what the author, Albert Camus (1913–60), called his 'cycle of the absurd' along with his essay *The Myth of Sisyphus* (*Le Mythe de Sisyphe*) and his play *Caligula*. A simple glimpse of the titles of the three works shows an emphasis on central characters who do not fit into positive heroic positions within their society but are outsiders, failures, monsters – or all these at once. French literature, at mid-century, was certainly itself not marginalized. The generation of authors who lived as adults during the Second World War produced six winners of the Nobel Prize in Literature (François Mauriac, 1952; Albert Camus, 1957; Saint-John Perse, 1960; Jean-Paul Sartre, who refused the award, 1964; Samuel Beckett, 1969; Claude Simon, 1985). This was a time, clearly, when French writers had captured the attention of the world. In some ways, they were all either themselves outsiders (four of them born outside of European France) or wrote memorably about outsiders (Mauriac in *Thérèse Desqueyroux*, 1927; Sartre in *La Nausée*, 1938).

## An unlikely hero

The title of *L'Etranger* designates its protagonist Meursault, a young man of modest condition and education, who works in an office in Algiers, and who, for no particular reason, shoots and kills a young Arab. The story, told in simple language in the first person singular, shows Meursault gradually growing in awareness of his distance from the society around him. The text is not formally a diary, but seems to be written from time to time, sometimes to note what has just happened and at others to present what the protagonist plans to do. There is a rather affectless quality to Meursault, particularly at the outset, though perhaps it is not so much a lack of emotion *per se* as a lack of the conventional dramatization and expression of emotions in their usual social form. The first sentence offers a good example:

> Today, Mama died. Or maybe yesterday. I don't know. I got a telegram from the nursing home: 'Mother deceased. Burial tomorrow. Respects.' That doesn't mean anything. It might have been yesterday.

> (*Aujourd'hui, maman est morte. Ou peut-être hier, je ne sais pas. J'ai reçu un télégramme de l'asile: 'Mère décédée. Enterrement demain. Sentiments distingués.' Cela ne veut rien dire. C'était peut-être hier.*)

In the simple declarative sentences, there is much attention to detail and especially sensation, with little explanation. We see the world from Meursault's point of view, that of a kind of Candide, like Céline's Bardamu, without a philosophy to follow or to combat (Meursault's narrative does make one wonder what Voltaire's *conte* would have been like as a first-person narrative). Meursault enjoys swimming, smoking, sunbathing, and sex with his girlfriend Marie. At an outing at the beach, Meursault, playing the peacemaker, takes a revolver from a friend who is threatening to kill an Arab with whom he has had a run-in, but later Meursault uses the gun to shoot the Arab. His account gives no place to fear or hostility, but rather to the heat, the blazing brightness of the sun.

The most remarkable moment of the novel is Meursault's discovery of himself just before his execution. Throughout the narrative, the protagonist-narrator seems to record what happens without thinking about it. There is such neutrality and such a lack of affect in his view of the world that he himself seems sometimes to be a person who is not there, almost a recording device. But his imprisonment and trial – he is tried for who he is rather than for the death of the Arab – make him aware of his difference from others, and in his revolt he becomes somebody, a self: 'Even when you're in the dock, it is interesting to hear people talking about yourself' (*Même sur un banc d'accusé, il est toujours intéressant d'entendre parler de soi*). He discovers his existence within the 'tender indifference of the world' (*la tendre indifférence du monde*), and he concludes by hoping that there would be many spectators when he is guillotined and that they would greet him with shouts of hatred. A personage almost without characteristics finally conceives of himself in a heroic dimension.

## The drama of just waiting

If Meursault becomes heroic only by affirming his status as outsider, Samuel Beckett's protagonists clearly occupy the outsider position from the start. Beckett (a truly bi-national and bi-lingual author, both Irish and French) differed, however, from Camus in distancing his characters from the everyday social world. Often, the unsympathetic central characters and their consciousness constitute the entire text, like the voice of *The Unnameable*, a novel (1953). The most accessible and best-known of Beckett's works is no doubt his two-act play *Waiting for Godot* (1952), with its tragicomic tramps or clowns, a play that for some critics typifies the 'theatre of the absurd', a term that was applied also to the plays of Beckett's contemporary Eugène Ionesco (1909–94), author of *The Bald Soprano* (*La Cantatrice chauve*, 1950) and *The Chairs* (*Les chaises*, 1952). Beckett manages the feat of making riveting drama out of two men waiting, in a bare landscape next to a tree, for the arrival of a certain 'Godot' whom they have never met. Where does all this happen? Could these two characters simply be described as inhabiting the author's consciousness?

**15. Lucien Raimbourg and Pierre Latour in Samuel Beckett's *En attendant Godot*, a photograph from the 1956 Paris production by Roger Blin**

The whole work has about it an air of barrenness and desolation that is accentuated by the simplicity of the language. Beckett said that he wrote in a foreign tongue to 'impoverish' and to 'discipline' himself, so that there would be no style or poetry to the text. Whether or not this was Beckett's actual reason for writing in French rather than in English, the argument could be made that throughout history poetry distinguished itself from ordinary discourse precisely by the acceptance of linguistic constraints. For most of the millennium of French literature, lyric poetry has been written in fixed forms of verse length and rhyme scheme that 'disciplined' the writer. In a similar vein, significant works like the medieval *Roman de la Rose* stripped away concrete secondary characteristics from its personae to concentrate both on what is most central to their story and what is most universal. Although the actors of *Waiting for Godot* cannot easily be interpreted as allegorical abstractions – into terms like 'hope', 'despair', 'reason', and so forth – their dialogue conveys a darkly comical version of human existence reduced to its most schematic.

Vladimir and Estragon, called Didi and Gogo, were perhaps in the same place the day before, waiting for the same person, together or not, wondering whether or not to wait, looking for ways to pass the time, and trying to decide what they will do the next day. While waiting, to fill the time, they discuss hanging themselves from the tree – Vladimir suggests that this would give them sexual pleasure. After a ridiculous discussion about how they could do this, they do nothing – doing nothing is the overarching principle. At the end of each of the two acts, they decide to leave and the stage directions indicate 'They don't move' (*Ils ne bougent pas*). In the midst of each act, another pair of characters shows up: Pozzo and his servant or slave Lucky. The hint of the circus in the clownish aspects of Vladimir and Estragon is reinforced by this new pair, since the whip-wielding Pozzo seems to be a ringmaster who can make his creature Lucky, whom he leads around on a rope, perform stunts – at least in the first act. By the second act, Pozzo is blind and does not remember anything that happened on the previous encounter the day before. Lucky, who entertains with a long, breathless, nonsensical speech in act I (suggesting, perhaps, the uselessness of learning, or even of all human achievement, including sport), is mute by act II.

In a text so enigmatic, so stripped down, the task of finding some link between what happens on stage and the world of life and ideas falls to the audience. Readers and critics have not tired of seizing on the most minute aspects of the play as the basis for exegesis. The most obvious issue is the meaning of 'Godot' – is he 'God', and, if so, what is the significance of the suffix, '-ot'? Is it a diminutive? Does it indicate contempt? Towards the end of each act, a boy comes to deliver the message that 'Monsieur Godot' will not be coming on this day but the next day instead. In each instance, the boy insists that he has not come before. By following Godot's request that they wait for him to come, have Vladimir and Estragon lost their ability to act and locked themselves into a prison of waiting? Or does the thought that Godot might someday come provide the only solace that Vladimir and Estragon have? Otherwise what is there?

The play is full of little gems of dark humour in almost epigrammatic forms that are hard to forget – whatever meaning we might assign. Estragon says to Vladimir, 'We always find something, eh, Didi, to give us the impression that we exist?' (*On trouve toujours quelque chose, hein, Didi, pour nous donner l'impression d'exister?*). This is an extraordinary question, on the part of a fictive character in a play. After all, the question of the characters' existence is traditionally posed, if at all, by the audience, usually in terms of questions such as 'Is this character believable?', that is, 'Could such a character have existed?'. This is the sort of thing that was debated in the 17th century about Corneille's heroes and heroines. Later, in regard to Beaumarchais's Figaro, the character seems to be bursting out of his role, thrusting aside the hierarchy to take a place that he merits by sheer excess of invention, activity, and desire. In a way – and this was clearly on the minds of the royal censors in the late 1770s – the danger was that Figaro, or his like, would become excessively real and no longer simply be amusing figures on stage but rather appear in the streets of Paris to demand their rights. So to have a central character of a play, like Estragon, so far from 'heroic' in the evaluative sense, call attention to the tenuousness of his own sense of existence is quite striking.

## The collapse and reinvention of character

This is not atypical of the times. The notion of character, like so many other concepts or practices of the literary tradition, was called into question quite energetically in the thirty years after the Second World War. This happens in a myriad of ways and in many genres. For instance, in Ionesco's *The Bald Soprano* (*La Cantatrice chauve*), the characters' identities collapse into a small set of names. Monsieur Smith and Madame Smith discuss someone named 'Bobby Watson', or so it seems at first, since 'Bobby Watson' proliferates. Madame Smith says that she was not thinking of Bobby Watson but rather:

> I was thinking of his wife. She had the same name as he did, Bobby, Bobby Watson. Since they had the same name, you couldn't tell them apart when you saw them together. It was only after his death that you could really tell which one was which.
>
> (*C'est à sa femme que je pense. Elle s'appelait comme lui, Bobby, Bobby Watson. Comme ils avaient le même nom, on ne pouvait pas les distinguer l'un de l'autre quand on les voyait ensemble. Ce n'est qu'après sa mort à lui, qu'on a pu vraiment savoir qui était l'un et qui était l'autre.*)

Superficially, this is a play that makes fun of the British middle class and also of the French view of the British middle class. But it is also, at the peak influence of French existentialism (with which Ionesco is not usually associated), a glimpse of a wider anxiety about personal identity, and, in the passage quoted, of women's existence. If the woman Bobby Watson could not be distinguished from her husband Bobby Watson until after the latter's death, the reason may be given in a book published, with great success, only a year before: Simone de Beauvoir's *The Second Sex* (*Le Deuxième sexe*, 1949). De Beauvoir (1908–86) reached a huge audience in this book that analyses the cultural myths of womanhood in specific roles: the young girl, the lesbian, the married woman, the mother, and so forth.

At the same time, in literary theory and criticism as well as in political and social thought, the concept of persona or role or agent or central narrative character became an object of much discussion and experimentation in the novel. This genre, which had seemed to harden into a 'classic' form at the end of the 19th century, had for decades been under attack. Paul Valéry, the poet and philosopher of literature, had in 1923 taken the novel to task for its lack of rigour, for its loose and baggy structure. In a striking formula, he complained in regard to Proust that the novel as genre had in common with dreams that they refused to take any responsibility for their structure: 'all their digressions belong' (*tous leurs écarts leur appartiennent*).

## Novels about novels

Two years after Valéry's stinging remark about the novel, André Gide (1869–1951) wrote a novel about writing a novel, *The Counterfeiters* (*Les Faux-monnayeurs*, 1925). The character Edouard is writing a novel with the same title as Gide's novel, and this title itself announces the criticism of the realist novel. This structure of a text reflected within itself, as if a series of boxes within boxes, is now widely known in French by a term of heraldic origin, *mise en abyme* (literally, 'placed in the chasm'). This critical reflection of the text upon the text became common in the years before the war and into the 1960s. In *Nausea* (*La Nausée*, 1938) by Jean-Paul Sartre (1905–80), the first-person narrator, a historian, reflects at length on the relation between writing and being, and at the end of the narrative decides to stop writing history and to write a novel instead – perhaps a novel something like the novel we are holding.

These influential early examples of reflexivity in the novel are the background to the major movement of formal experimentation in what is called the *nouveau roman* ('new novel'), a term popularized by Alain Robbe-Grillet in his 1963 essay *For a New Novel* (*Pour un nouveau roman*). The term *nouveau roman* was apparently first used to describe this kind of writing by Émile Henriot in a negative review of Robbe-Grillet's novel *La Jalousie* (*Jealousy*, 1957; the term *jalousie* also means a window blind). *La*

*Jalousie* illustrates the ways in which the *nouveau roman* called into question the notion of central character, along with many other conventions attributed to the traditional novel.

*La Jalousie* is narrated by a nameless character. In fact, the verb 'narrate' may be misleading in this case, since the overall story is never really told but may be pieced together by the reader from what appear to be overlapping, sometimes repetitive, sometimes contradictory, fragments that are more like description (they are in the present tense) than storytelling. The persons named in *La Jalousie* are A…, Franck, and the latter's wife Christiane. Gradually it becomes clear that the narrator supposes a love affair between A… and Franck. We can infer – from notations telling us that four places have been set at the dinner table, but that Christiane will not be coming, etc. – that this narrator is a jealous husband. This text amply justifies the term *école du regard* ('school of the gaze') which was also used to designate the *nouveau roman*. Here is a typical passage:

> In the banana plantation behind them, a trapezoidal section stretches uphill where, because no clusters have yet been harvested since the suckers were planted, the quincunxes are still perfectly regular.
>
> (*Dans la bananeraie, derrière eux, une pièce en forme de trapèze s'étend vers l'amont, dans laquelle, aucun régime n'ayant encore été récolté depuis la plantation des souches, la régularité des quinconces est encore absolue.*)

The objects and events described are deliberately banal: table settings, the sound of a truck climbing an incline, the stain on the wall from a crushed millipede, the windows, hands on a table.

Although the source of these descriptions is never named, it – or rather, he, the husband – is not disembodied since there is heavy insistence on the point of view, in the literal sense that certain things are visible or not given the distance, angle, and lighting conditions specified in the text. The narrator's characteristics can also be inferred from what he notices, from the terms and precision of his description, from the obsessive return to certain moments and to certain traits that he notices in A. . . . Yet, other than through this effort at description of the physical world, we have no access to the thoughts of any of the characters, only a series of clues. The paradoxical situation of a central character who is both everywhere and yet, explicitly, nowhere, shows the extreme effort to renew the representation of the central persona, who is far from a 'hero', yet fundamental to the existence of the fiction itself.

Such inventive stretching of the category of the protagonist is common among Robbe-Grillet's contemporaries. In *Second Thoughts* (*La Modification*, 1957), a novel by Michel Butor (1926– ) that appeared the same year as *La Jalousie*, the protagonist (who is also the presumed narrator, as well as the presumed reader) is simply 'you' (*vous* – if we assume that the narrator and the protagonist are the same person, the choice of the formal pronoun adds another layer of strange distance from the self). At the outset of the story, the effect is quite strong: 'You've put your left foot on the copper groove, and with your right shoulder you vainly attempt to push the sliding door a bit more'. And in *The Golden Fruits* (*Les fruits d'or*, 1963) by Nathalie Sarraute (1900–99), the continuity usually given to a novel by the protagonists is instead assured by the topic of a multitude of conversations about a novel also called *Les fruits d'or* – another *mise en abyme* like Gide's *Les Faux-monnayeurs*.

At the same time, lyric poetry, which has often been in the forefront of attempts to expand the concepts of character and voice, pushed even further in complicating these components of the text. In Yves Bonnefoy's *On the Motion and Immobility of Douve* (*Du mouvement et de l'immobilité de Douve*, 1953), an 'I' sometimes addresses an entity named 'Douve' (grammatically feminine) who seems to have human features but also to become at times a landscape, an animal, and various other objects. Lyric poetry has often displayed its characters situated in, and particularized by, an environment, but Bonnefoy goes much further. Douve seems to be aggressed by the places in which she is located (and the choice of the pronoun 'she' confers a humanness that is not at all certain in this poem). By making up the proper noun 'Douve', Bonnefoy invites the reader to wonder which of the meanings of the French noun *douve* is most pertinent: the moat of a castle, a flowering plant (the Spearwort), a parasitic worm, or a stave. The strong association of character with place unites the lyric poetry of this period with other genres, such as the cinema.

## Character and place

Often associated with the *nouveau roman*, Marguerite Duras (born Marguerite Donnadieu in Indo-China, 1914; died in Paris in 1996) wrote the scenario for the film *Hiroshima mon amour* (directed by Alain Resnais, 1959) and published it separately as a book in 1960. Writers in this period moved often from novel to film and back – after her collaboration with Resnais, Duras herself later directed a score of films, as did Robbe-Grillet after writing the screenplay for Renais's *Last Year at Marienbad* (*L'Année dernière à Marienbad*, 1961). The screenplays, published in book form, are scarcely distinguishable from many other novels of the period that were not filmed nor even meant to be filmed, such as *Jealousy*. As printed texts, these screenplays are clearly part of French literature, and *Hiroshima mon amour* illustrates the close relationship between the construction (or deconstruction) of a main human character and the evocation of the destruction of Hiroshima by an American nuclear bomb in 1945.

Just as the character of Hugo's *Notre Dame de Paris* is as much the cathedral as the human character, Quasimodo, the bell-ringer, who gives the cathedral a voice, so in Duras's screenplay the nameless French actress who plays the role of a nurse in a film about Hiroshima and the Japanese architect who becomes her

**16. A scene from Alain Resnais's film _Hiroshima mon amour_ (1959)**

lover exist almost exclusively to give voice to the experience of the destruction of Hiroshima and the wartime occupation of the city of Nevers in France. She tells the Japanese man a story that she had never told anyone before about her love, as an adolescent, for a German soldier. She and the soldier planned to marry, but he was killed by the French resistance and she was punished by her family, her head was shaved, and she was locked in a cold cellar for months. When her family released her, she bicycled to Paris during the night, and it was in Paris that she saw the newspaper headline announcing the bombing of Hiroshima. He tells her that she has seen nothing in Hiroshima: 'You have seen _nothing_ in Hiroshima. Nothing' (_Tu n'as_ rien _vu à Hiroshima. Rien_). She insists 'I have seen _everything_. Everything' (_J'ai_ tout _vu. Tout._). And this statement is accompanied in the screenplay by filming directions for flashbacks to the hospital, to the museum, to photographs of the city right after the bombing. The unrepresentability of the destruction in language or in images runs throughout the dialogue of the two lovers. Though the woman's experience in Nevers is easier to describe, it too is a taboo subject at this time. The massive French collaboration with the German occupying forces was a subject almost never mentioned in French media until Marcel Ophuls's *Le Chagrin et la pitié* ten years later.

Duras's characters are believable, yet opaque. They are what they say, and what they say is about love and destruction. The force of the screenplay is in large part the incantatory dialogue, which slides from apparently realistic conversation to something far from ordinary speech, like the actress's repeated utterance: 'You kill me. You do me good' (*Tu me tues. Tu me fais du bien*), one of the most explicit voicings of an erotic view of war, colonialism, and the relation of cultures that is ubiquitous in Duras's work, and appears, indeed, in other novels and screenplays of the late 1950s, when France was gradually and painfully losing its colonies. At the end of the filmplay, Duras makes explicit the identification of the man and the woman with their cities. The French woman looks at her lover – the stage directions note 'They look at each other without seeing' – and says 'You are Hi-ro-shi-ma', to which he replies, 'That is my name. Yes. [That is only as far as we have come still. And we will stay there forever.] And your name is Nevers. Ne-vers-in-Fran-ce' (*Hi-ro-shi-ma. C'est ton nom.—C'est mon nom. Oui. [On en est là seulement encore. Et on en restera là pour toujours.] Ton nom à toi est Nevers. Ne-vers-en-Fran-ce*). Duras here approaches the allegorical use of character most prominent in the Middle Ages and then glimpsed again in Bonnefoy's poetry.

# Chapter 9

# French-speaking heroes without borders?

In the last two decades of the 20th century and the first decade of the 21st, the grand old men of the Second World War generation left the stage of French literature to a new cast of writers, with new concerns. The many novelists among these contemporaries generally leave behind the formal experimentation of the *nouveau roman*. Many of these authors, such as Antonine Maillet (1929– ), Maryse Condé (born Beaucolon, 1930– ), Hélène Cixous (1937– ), Assia Djebar (Fatima-Zohra Imalayène, 1936– ), Daniel Pennac (1944– ), Raphaël Confiant (1951– ), Patrick Chamoiseau (1953– ), and Michel Houellebecq (Michel Houellebecq, born 1956, Michel Thomas, la Réunion), and Calixthe Beyala (1961– ), were, like their predecessors Marguerite Yourcenar (1903–87, born Marguerite Cleenewerck de Crayencour), Albert Camus (1913–60), Saint-John Perse (1887–1975), and Claude Simon (1913–2005), born outside of continental France – the French *Métropole*, or the 'Hexagon', as it is often called. Others were born within the Hexagon: Annie Ernaux (1940– ), J. M. G. Le Clézio (1940– ), Didier Daeninckx (1949– ), Marie NDiaye (1967– ), and Marie Darrieussecq (1969– ).

## Francophone writers, or writers in French?

Most of these authors have in common that they manifest a paradoxical shrinking and expansion of French literature. The France of the turn of the 21st century had lost a number of its colonies (Algeria, Indo-China, Morocco) but still sees its cultural sphere, its 'soft power', grow, as the French are among the most outspoken in claiming to resist the influence of United States culture. For the last several decades, it has been common to describe some of these authors – for instance, Maillet, Condé, and Chamoiseau – as 'francophone' writers, while others – such as Cixous, Houellebecq, and Camus – were never classified as such, though all of them were born outside European France. Who is, or what is, a 'francophone' writer? And is there a 'francophone literature'? According to the authoritative French dictionary, *Le Trésor de la langue française*, the term, which dates to 1932, simply means someone 'who speaks French' (*[Celui, celle] qui parle le français*), but in English-speaking universities the term has been used almost exclusively to designate writers from Africa, the Caribbean, and North America. It is undeniable that much of the vitality of today's literature in French comes from the recognition of such important writers as Léopold Sédar Senghor, Ousmane Sembène, Cheikh Hamidou Kane, and Birago Diop from Senegal; Ahmadou Kourouma from the Côte d'Ivoire; Driss Chraïbi and Tahar Ben Jelloun from Morocco; Roger Dorsinville and René Depestre from Haiti; and many others who have in common both the French language and the experience or cultural memory of French colonial culture. But questions remain as to the conceptual framework within which such writers are to be situated.

On 16 March 2007, the Parisian newspaper *Le Monde* published a manifesto entitled 'For a "world-literature" in French' (*Pour une 'littérature-monde' en français*), signed by a group of 44 influential writers. In it, they declare that that year marked the 'End of francophone [literature]. And [the] birth of a world-literature in French' (*Fin de la francophonie. Et naissance d'une littérature-monde en français*). There are different ways of looking at how such a distinguished group of 'francophone' authors came to the point of announcing the end of the literature that had brought them to the attention of a wide public. One could say that the academic concept of 'francophone literature' – conceived by its promoters primarily as a way of creating greater inclusiveness within the study of literature in French – had been such a great success that it outgrew its usefulness. One could also say that the concept of 'francophone literature' collapsed under the weight of its own inconsistencies and incoherence. And, finally, one could say that the term seemed racist and insulting to many of the authors to whom it was applied. As Tahar Ben Jelloun (1944– ), the Paris-based Moroccan writer, has said:

> To be considered francophone is to be an alien, someone who comes from elsewhere and who is told to stay in an assigned place somewhat off to the side of 'true' French writers [*écrivains français de souche*].
>
> '*La cave de ma mémoire, le toit de ma maison sont des mots français*', in *Pour une littérature-monde*, ed. Michel Le Bris and Jean Rouaud (Paris: Gallimard, 2007), p. 117.

And these various explanations are not incompatible.

There will always be reasons to sort literature into a multitude of categories, including the region in which a text is written; the period; the gender, class, race, religion, sexuality, or political affiliation of its author; the formal or generic characteristics of the text itself; the mode of diffusion or publication; and so forth. At the turn of the century, a major thematic consensus among writers in French is that the apparently stable categories of identity for individuals, nations, and other groups no longer can be taken for granted, including *francophonie* – not that boundaries and belonging are themselves outmoded, but that they have exploded exponentially and are now the source of endless variations of authorial and narratorial voices and of protagonists.

## A novel from history with a new voice

Let us consider, for example, a very successful historical novel by a French author from Guadeloupe, Maryse Condé (1930– )

*I, Tituba, Black Witch of Salem* (*Moi, Tituba, sorcière noire de Salem*, 1987), in which the protagonist and narrator is an African slave brought from Barbados to the colony of New England and tried as a witch in 1692. Orphaned as an infant and chased off the plantation to die in the forest, she is raised by an African woman healer to learn of herbal medicine and of communicating with the dead. Not a slave, for she was chased away rather than sold, she looks at life differently from her African compatriots, but she accepts to become a slave from love. She follows her husband when he is sold and sent from Barbados to Boston. The character Tituba is founded on a real person, about whom Condé gathered all she could from the archives of the witch trials of late 17th-century Massachusetts (Condé has given Tituba African ancestry, though this is not the prevailing view among historians). But in trying to give Tituba the biography that was never written – or rather, the autobiography that she never wrote or that did not survive – Condé clearly writes for a late-20th-century reader who will necessarily think in modern terms. Tituba uses the terms 'racism' and 'feminism' to describe outlooks and practices, the first to describe the world as it really was and the second to evoke an aspiration that Condé supposes women of the time must have felt. The character-narrator Tituba is a person of the imagination in more than one sense. She is not simply a version of an historical figure as Condé imagines her, but Tituba is also a character with the gift of imagination or vision to look forward to the future, a kind of Maryse Condé in reverse. As a wise woman, or 'sorcerer', Tituba can see and communicate with the dead but also with those who are alive after her own death.

*Moi, Tituba* clearly exceeds any bounds of the 'francophone' novel – it is not surprising, therefore, that Maryse Condé signed the 2007 manifesto. It is a work in French that does not represent a French-speaking culture but rather the English-speaking colonial world of the 17th century. Tituba, an English speaker, tells her story in French without any apology. The work often refers to other literary traditions; for instance, Hester, the heroine of Nathaniel Hawthorne's *The Scarlet Letter* (1850) makes a surprising appearance as a friend and perhaps lover of Tituba. The other characters, good and bad, are British, American colonials, African slaves or Caribbean-born slaves of African and mixed European-African descent (like Tituba herself, a child born of her mother's rape by an English sailor on board the ship *Christ the King*), and Portuguese Jews.

A consistent and very explicit aspect of Tituba's values and personality is her resistance to the appeal of vengeance, even in the face of repeated and extreme violence, such as the execution (the murder) of her mother for having resisted a plantation owner who attempted to rape her. Equally important is her refusal to accept the split into placative 'happy slave' exterior self and cynical but 'free' inner self – a stance adopted by her husband John Indian. Implicitly, Tituba conveys the view that this claim to inner 'freedom' is itself a deformity that debases the person and prevents any real happiness.

## The metamorphosis of the heroine

'Witch' is a term applied to women usually to insult or to threaten, but Condé has turned things around by making Tituba a real heroine, clearly implying approval of Tituba by the reader. A still more unlikely reframing of roles takes place in Marie Darieussecq's *Pig Tales* (1996 – the French title *Truismes* is a play on the word 'truism' and the word *truie*, 'sow'), where the narrator-heroine finds herself being transformed into a sow. Darieussecq (1969– ) has written something resembling Voltaire's *conte philosophique* and Kafka's 'Metamorphosis' but with a voice that is unique in its self-deprecating naïveté. While the feminist premise might seem rather obvious (i.e. that men both view and treat women like 'sows' – one of the infinite number of insulting terms for women, particularly in terms of their sexuality), making the conceit unfold is a *tour de force*. To take the metaphor of the *truie* and literalize it into a fantasy set in a very realistic modern world is particularly difficult to do within a first-person narrative. Unlike Kafka's Gregor Samsa, whose definitive transformation into a cockroach has already occurred at the start of the story, Darieussecq's nameless young woman morphs into and out of her piggish form gradually, and the boundary line of her interactions with the male characters is also fluctuating and indistinct.

As she becomes more of a pig, she finds her sexual appetite increasing, and in the 'beauty parlour' in which she works as a masseuse (in fact, as a prostitute), her new sexual aggressiveness attracts a more animalistic clientele, though her increasingly pig-like skin, nose, and bristles eventually put an end to her domestic and professional arrangements. As the protagonist recounts her experiences in a naive way – actually, even less judgemental than Candide – Darieussecq explores the ambivalences of male attitudes towards sex as well as the corruption of the political system. The author cleverly weaves together cultural references and humour, even recalling the legend of the werewolf that was Marie de France's focus in *Bisclavret* eight centuries before, when the protagonist falls in love with a werewolf named Yvan (the name seems deliberately chosen to recall the medieval Breton repertory).

## A critique of Western society

The final happy note of *Truismes* – the heroine has decided to remain a pig because 'it's more practical for living in the forest' where she has found a mate, a boar who is 'very beautiful and very virile' – contrasts with an unrelentingly downbeat *succès de scandale* that appeared eight years earlier and to which the adjective 'piggish' might well apply: *Atomised* (*Les particules élémentaires*, 1998, published in the US as *The Elementary Particles*) by Michel Houellebecq. One of the two protagonists in fact sees himself in a dream 'in the form of a young pig with plump, smooth skin'. This third-person narrative is multi-tonal, including an academic biographical account of one of its two protagonists, half-brothers, raised separately. One, the biologist Michel, leads a virtually asexual life dedicated to genetic research, while the other, Bruno, a *lycée* teacher of French literature, sees sex as his only reason for living. Their different paths bring them unhappiness and ruin the lives of any women who approach them. And the narrative itself manages to make everything it touches seem repulsive: science, religion, food, sex, friendship. The whole account is threaded with portentous 'scientific' statements about the end of Christian belief and the advent of a deterministic, materialist worldview. Michel's childhood girlfriend, who loves him and whom he rebuffs in adolescence, is described as she blossoms into the beauty that dooms her:

> From the age of thirteen years onward, under the influence of progesterone and estradiol secreted by her ovaries, fatty cushions are deposited at the level of a girl's breasts and buttocks. These organs, in the best of cases, acquire a full, harmonious, round aspect.

The voices of the narrator and of each of the male protagonists, who are given to long monologues on science, determinism, religion, anthropology, and social values, all advance the view that Western societies are in a state of advanced decay due to the rise of sexual freedom and of individualism and the decline of Christianity and of the family – in all of this 1974 is identified as the *annus horribilis*. To the extent that he intersperses long philosophical discourses with sexual details (Bruno, for instance, masturbates in quite disruptive ways), Houllebecq's work resembles Sade. On the other hand, it is very unclear what message might be taken from this book, despite its relentless didacticism. Yet Houellebecq is very much of his time in terms of the broad cultural mood. *Les particules élémentaires* appeared two years before the 'millennium', when a sense of foreboding was widespread. The media had warned that a glitch in computer code, the 'Y2K bug', would paralyse airports, banks, and even household appliances. Meanwhile, fundamentalist religious movements, of many origins, were building up the aggressive energy that led to elections of candidates from the Christian and Islamic right, in their respective spheres of influence.

## And a critique of the East

In contrast to Houellebecq's relentless misery with its implicit appeal for an authoritarian reimposition of social values in the hope of eliminating individual choice and collective alienation, Amélie Nothomb (1967– ) at the same moment published a novel with a joyous celebration of European individualism and self-responsibility in the context of precisely the type of paternalist system that, at times, *Les particules élémentaires* seems to value. In *Fear and Trembling* (*Stupeur et tremblements*, 1999), she tells the first-person story of Amélie, a Belgian born in Japan and fluent in Japanese, who comes to work for a large Japanese corporation. The mood of Nothomb's novel is entirely different from the dark, angular, jarring spirit of Duras's *Hiroshima mon amour*, but it has in common with that screenplay the portrayal of the relation between civilizations in terms of individuals and their erotic fascination for one another (we recall the refrain in Duras's text, 'You kill me. You do me good.'). In Nothomb's novel, Amélie is obsessed with the beauty of the Japanese woman who supervises her and who assigns increasingly demeaning tasks, until the Belgian protagonist has no other responsibility than to clean the male and female toilets of the forty-fourth floor of the Yumimoto corporate headquarters. In Amélie's ironic pleasure at the complete misuse of her talents as translator and business strategist, the individual erotic attachment to the supervisor, Fubuki Mori, and the broader cultural fascination – that is, the fascination of Western cultures with the mysterious East – cannot be separated. Therefore, descriptive passages reveal as much about the education and desires of the narrator as about their object, and in this one the allegorical turn is signalled by a reference to one of the best-known passages in Pascal's *Pensées*:

Two meters before me, the spectacle of her face was captivating.
Her eyelids lowered on the numbers kept her from seeing that
I was studying her. She had the most beautiful nose in the world,
the Japanese nose, this inimitable nose, with the delicate nostrils,
that one can recognize among thousands. Not all Japanese have this
nose, but anyone who has this nose must be Japanese. If Cleopatra
had had this nose, the geography of the planet would have been all
shaken up.

## The theme that will not go away: the Second World War

The limits of the 'francophone' but also the boundaries of
acceptable protagonists are challenged aggressively in *Les
Bienveillantes* (2006), winner not only of the prestigious Prix
Goncourt but also the Grand prix du roman from the Académie
Française. The author is Jonathan Littel, born in New York
in 1967 and a citizen of the United States at the time of the
publication (he subsequently also obtained French citizenship,
although he does not live in France). The oddity of an American
winning these prizes would no doubt have provoked controversy
in itself, but for an author of Jewish ancestry to write a novel
from the point of view of a Nazi SS officer, who himself assists
in killing Jews, was considered by many to be quite outrageous,
particularly because there is some effort to make the narrator
'sympathetic' when contrasted with more enthusiastic killers.
Maximilien Aue, the protagonist, in an account of how he wrote
his memoirs, mentions off-handedly a long-standing tendency to
vomit after meals and says that he prefers work to leisure because
work keeps him from thinking about the war (perhaps Littel's
study of Pascal in a French *lycée* brings this echo of comments
in the *Pensées* about keeping busy to avoid thinking about the
important things). Aue runs a lace-making factory, is a married
father of twins, and aims at outward bourgeois respectability to
cover his homosexuality and to make his shame from the war
fade away.

Littel's novel is highly conventional in its form, especially when compared to the experimentation of the *nouveau roman* decades before. It seems that one of the major creative efforts in recent French novels is to conceive unusual protagonists whose first-person narratives stretch various boundaries of identity, with emphasis on national as well as sexual and racial identity.

There is no better representative of the movement for a 'world literature' in French than J. M. G. (Jean-Marie Gustave) Le Clézio, whose novel *Ritournelle de la faim* (*The refrain of hunger*) appeared in October 2008 just as the author became the latest French-language writer to win the Nobel Prize in Literature. The presentation speech given by a member of the selection committee before the Swedish Academy began with this question:

> Of what use are characters to a literary work? Roland Barthes maintained that the most antiquated of all literary conventions was the proper name – the Peter, Paul, and Anna who never existed but whom we are expected to take seriously and feel concerned about when we read novels.

Le Clézio began his writing career when this view prevailed, yet from his very first novel, *The Interrogation* (*Le Procès-verbal*, 1963), has shown the world through the eyes of his protagonists, who are often, like Adam Pollo of *The Interrogation*, outsiders to the world that they so sharply observe. Le Clézio's narratives concern a wide variety of places: Africa, in *Desert* (1980) and *Onitsha* (1991); Mauritius – home of his ancestors – in *The Prospector* (*Le Chercheur d'or*, 1985) and *The Quarantine* (*La Quarantaine*, 1995); Palestine in *Wandering Star* (*Étoile errante*, 1996); and Latin America, in *Ourania* (2006). He shows an immense ability to imagine the world from the point of view of his many characters, but Le Clézio, in keeping with the trend in French novels over the past decades, has moved from highly experimental, often difficult to follow narratives, to more straightforward stories.

Whereas in *The Interrogation* the main character, who is sometimes also the narrator, is insane, *Ritournelle de la faim* follows Ethel, a fairly ordinary protagonist, from 1931, when she is ten years old, until the end of the Second World War. But in both of these novels, separated by 45 years, the characters are connected in multiple ways to the world overseas. Adam Pollo seems to have just returned from serving in the French army during the Algerian Revolution, while Ethel's parents are from Mauritius and her story begins with her favourite memory, a visit with her beloved grand-uncle to the Colonial Exposition in 1931. As the Nobel presentation notes, Le Clézio's work 'belongs to the tradition of the critique of civilisation, which on French ground can be traced back to Chateaubriand, Bernardin de Saint-Pierre, Diderot, and [...] Montaigne'. In this respect, Le Clézio is highly representative both of his own time, a period of post-colonial criticism and debates about national and linguistic identity. His work is therefore a good place to enter into French literature, both in its origins and in its persistent variations.

## Endless encounters

As we have seen, the literary tradition in French both roots texts in their original historical moment and allows them to encounter one another across the centuries. Texts, in other words, are a bit like the water lilies of Claude Monet's famous series of paintings, the *Nympheas* (1906–27). The lilies are rooted separately in the soil at the bottom of the pond but drift on their stems so that the leaves and flowers shift and touch on the water surface. Just as Le Clézio's work encounters Bernardin's and Montaigne's across the space of hundreds of years, so also Darrieussecq's depiction of the shifting boundary between animality and humanity intersects with the *Lais* of Marie de France, while Proust's novel frequently refers to the writers of the 17th century. Houellebecq's work has resemblances to the moralist tradition of Pascal and La Bruyère, and Yves Bonnefoy weaves into his poetry echoes of Baudelaire.

Such encounters will certainly continue, and there will surely be surprises to come as writers formerly separated by vast distances find themselves in close proximity thanks to shifts in the book trade that make it easy for a reader in Québec to purchase a book by a writer from Senegal or Algeria. France has also been in the forefront of development of cultural resources on the internet. The Bibliothèque Nationale de France makes tens of thousands of books available online, while radio stations like France Culture and France Inter make readings of literary texts and discussions of literature available for download.

Just as important as the increased diffusion of French literary culture is the widespread perception that French intellectual culture is the single most significant alternative, at least among Western nations, to the English-speaking world. For some people, the notion of an 'alternative' easily slides into the idea of an 'opposition', and thus implies hostility and struggle. For many other people, including perhaps the readers of this book, the French literary tradition offers a welcome new vantage point from which to see the world, past and present. In a world threatened by sameness, we have never had a greater need for the French *différence*.

# Further reading

## General

Wendy Ayres-Bennett, *A History of the French Language Through Texts* (London: Routledge, 1996).

Peter France (ed.), *New Oxford Companion to Literature in French* (Oxford: Clarendon Press, 1995).

Denis Hollier (ed.), *A New History of French Literature* (Cambridge, MA: Harvard University Press, 1989).

Colin Jones, *The Cambridge Illustrated History of France* (Cambridge: Cambridge University Press, 1999).

Sarah Kay, Terence Cave, and Malcolm Bowie, *A Short History of French Literature* (Oxford: Oxford University Press, 2003).

Eva Martin Sartori (ed.), *The Feminist Encyclopedia of French Literature* (Westport, CT.: Greenwood Press, 1999).

Sonya Stephens (ed.), *A History of Women's Writing in France* (Cambridge: Cambridge University Press, 2000).

## Medieval and Renaissance

Barbara K. Altman and Deborah McGrady (eds.), *Christine de Pizan: A Casebook* (New York: Routledge, 2003).

Simon Gaunt, *Retelling the Tale: An Introduction to French Medieval Literature* (London: Duckworth, 2001).

Sarah Kay, *The chansons de geste in the Age of Romance: Political Fictions* (Oxford: Clarendon Press, 1995).

Sarah Kay, *The Troubadours: An Introduction* (Cambridge: Cambridge University Press, 1999).

Neil Kenny, *An Introduction to Sixteenth-Century French Literature and Thought: Other Times, Other Places* (London: Duckworth, 2008).

R. J. Knecht, *Renaissance Warrior and Patron: The Reign of Francis I* (Cambridge: Cambridge University Press, 1994).

Ullrich Langer, *The Cambridge Companion to Montaigne* (Cambridge: Cambridge University Press, 2005).

John Lyons and Mary McKinley, *Critical Tales: New Studies of the Heptameron and Early Modern Culture* (Philadelphia, PA: University of Pennsylvania Press, 1993).

Deborah McGrady, *Controlling Readers: Guillaume de Machaut and His Late Medieval Audience* (Toronto: University of Toronto Press, 2007).

Michael Randall, *The Gargantuan Polity: On the Individual and the Community in the French Renaissance* (Toronto and London: University of Toronto Press, 2008).

Jane Taylor, *The Poetry of François Villon* (Cambridge: Cambridge University Press, 2001).

## 17th and 18th centuries

Faith E. Beasley, *Salons, History, and the Creation of 17th-Century France* (Aldershot and Burlington: Ashgate Publishing, 2006).

Jean-Claude Bonnet, *Naissance du Panthéon: Essai sur le culte des Grands Hommes* (Paris: Fayard, 1998).

Peter Brooks, *The Novel of Worldliness: Crébillon, Marivaux, Laclos, Stendhal* (Princeton, NJ: Princeton University Press, 1969).

Robert Darnton, *The Forbidden Best-Sellers of Pre-Revolutionary France* (New York: W. W. Norton, 1995).

Joan DeJean, *Tender Geographies: Women and the Origins of the Novel in France* (New York: Columbia University Press, 1991).

William Doyle, *The French Revolution: A Very Short Introduction* (Oxford: Oxford University Press, 2001).

Anne E. Duggan, *Salonnières, Furies, and Fairies: The Politics of Gender and Cultural Change in Absolutist France* (Newark, DE: University of Delaware Press, 2005).

James F. Gaines, *Social Structures in Molière's Theater* (Columbus, OH: Ohio State University Press, 1984).

Dena Goodman, *The Republic of Letters: A Cultural History of the French Enlightenment* (Ithaca, NY: Cornell University Press, 1996).

Michael Moriarty, *Early Modern French Thought: The Age of Suspicion* (Oxford: Oxford University Press, 2003).

Michael Moriarty, *Fallen Nature, Fallen Selves: Early Modern French Thought II* (Oxford: Oxford University Press, 2006).

Orest Ranum, *Paris in the Age of Absolutism: An Essay* (University Park, PA: Pennsylvania State University Press, 2002).

Lewis Carl Seifert, *Fairy Tales, Sexuality, and Gender in France, 1690–1715: Nostalgic Utopias* (Cambridge: Cambridge University Press, 1996).

## 19th century

Tim Farrant, *An Introduction to Nineteenth-Century French Literature* (London: Duckworth, 2007).

Alison Finch, *Women's Writing in Nineteenth-Century France* (Cambridge: Cambridge University Press, 2000).

Cheryl L. Krueger, *The Art of Procrastination: Baudelaire's Poetry in Prose* (Newark, DE: University of Delaware Press, 2007).

Rosemary Lloyd (ed.), *The Cambridge Companion to Baudelaire* (Cambridge: Cambridge University Press, 2005).

Christopher Prendergast, *Paris and the Nineteenth Century* (Oxford: Blackwell, 1992).

Debarati Sanyal, *The Violence of Modernity: Baudelaire, Irony and the Politics of Form* (Baltimore, MD: Johns Hopkins University Press, 2006).

David Wakefield, *The French Romantics: Literature and the Visual Arts 1800–1840* (London: Chaucer Press, 2007).

## 20th and 21st centuries

Lucille Frackman Becker, *Twentieth-Century French Women Novelists* (Boston, MA: G. K. Hall, 1989).

Victoria Best, *An Introduction to Twentieth-Century French Literature* (London: Duckworth, 2002).

Dorothy Blair, *Senegalese Literature in French* (Boston, MA: Twayne Publishers, 1984).

Patrick Corcoran, *The Cambridge Introduction to Francophone Literature* (Cambridge: Cambridge University Press, 2007).

Edward J. Hughes, *Writing Marginality in Modern French Literature, from Loti to Genet* (Cambridge: Cambridge University Press, 2001).

Ann Jefferson, *Biography and the Question of Literature in France* (New York: Oxford University Press, 2007).

Shirley Ann Jordan, *Contemporary French Women's Writing: Women's Visions, Women's Voices* (Bern: Peter Lang, 2005).

Michael Lucey, *Never Say I: Sexuality and the First Person in Colette, Gide, and Proust* (Durham, NC: Duke University Press, 2006).

Christopher L. Miller, *Nationalists and Nomads: Essays on Francophone African Literature and Culture* (Chicago, IL: University of Chicago Press, 1998).

Charles Sowerwine, *France since 1870: Culture, Politics and Society* (Basingstoke and New York: Palgrave, 2001).

# Index

Index

Index

# HISTORY
## A Very Short Introduction
John H. Arnold

*History: A Very Short Introduction* is a stimulating essay about how we understand the past. The book explores various questions provoked by our understanding of history, and examines how these questions have been answered in the past. Using examples of how historians work, the book shares the sense of excitement at discovering not only the past, but also ourselves.

> 'A stimulating and provocative introduction to one of collective humanity's most important quests – understanding the past and its relation to the present. A vivid mix of telling examples and clear cut analysis.'
>
> **David Lowenthal, University College London**

> 'This is an extremely engaging book, lively, enthusiastic and highly readable, which presents some of the fundamental problems of historical writing in a lucid and accessible manner. As an invitation to the study of history it should be difficult to resist.'
>
> **Peter Burke, Emmanuel College, Cambridge**

www.oup.co.uk/vsi/history

# ROUSSEAU
## A Very Short Introduction
Robert Wokler

Rousseau was both a central figure of the European Enlightenment and its most formidable critic. In this study of his life, works, sources, and influence, Robert Wokler shows how Rousseau's account of the trappings of civilization across a wide range of disciplines was inspired by ideals of humanity's self-realization in a condition of unfettered freedom.

> 'Remarkably well-informed . . . this at once chronological and thematic treatment of Rousseau's thought makes plain its unity and coherence. Addressing both philosophical and political sources as well as influences, the work includes a fine bibliographical commentary . . . and commends itself through the clarity of its exposition and the rigour of its analysis.'
>
> **Raymond Trousson, *Dix-huitieme siecle***

> 'One of the best-informed, most balanced, short general introductions to Rousseau . . . in English. . . . Wokler's study leaves a vivid impression of Rousseau's uniqueness and originality as a thinker.'
>
> **Graeme Garrard, *History of Political Thought***

www.oup.co.uk/isbn/0-19-280198-8

# DADA AND SURREALISM
## A Very Short Introduction
David Hopkins

The avant-garde movements of Dada and Surrealism continue to have a huge influence on cultural practice, especially in contemporary art. In this new treatment of the subject, David Hopkins focuses on the many debates surrounding these movements: the Marquis de Sade's Surrealist deification, issues of quality (How good is Dali?), the idea of the 'readymade', attitudes towards the city and the impact of Freud.

Hopkins explores the international nature of these movements and the huge range of media employed by both Dada and Surrealism. He also examines the Dadaist obsession with the body-as-mechanism in relation to the Surrealists' return to the fetishized/eroticized body.

http://www.oup.co.uk/isbn/0-19-280254-2

# ONLINE CATALOGUE
## A Very Short Introduction

Our online catalogue is designed to make it easy to find your ideal Very Short Introduction. View the entire collection by subject area, watch author videos, read sample chapters, and download reading guides.

http://fds.oup.com/www.oup.co.uk/general/vsi/index.html

# SOCIAL MEDIA
# Very Short Introduction

# Join our community
www.oup.com/vsi

- Join us online at the official Very Short Introductions
  **Facebook** page.
- Access the thoughts and musings of our authors with our
  online **blog**.
- Sign up for our monthly **e-newsletter** to receive information
  on all new titles publishing that month.
- Browse the full range of Very Short Introductions online.
- Read **extracts** from the Introductions for free.
- Visit our library of **Reading Guides**. These guides, written by our
  expert authors will help you to question again, why you think
  what you think.
- If you are a teacher or lecturer you can order inspection
  copies quickly and simply via our website.